«

IT HAS TRULY BEEN
A GREAT SUCCESS,
NOT FOR THE
APPLAUSE, BUT FOR
THE ASTONISHMENT,
THE BAFFLEMENT, THE
EXASPERATION AND THE
DISMAY I CAUSED THE
AUDIENCE. YOU DON'T
KNOW HOW MUCH
I ENJOYED IT!

»

LUIGI PIRANDELLO

Design:
Goto Design, New York

Editors:
Valentina Castellani and Alison McDonald

Publication Coordinator:
Emily Florido

Gagosian Gallery Coordinators:
Darlina Goldak, Nicole Heck, Kim Higby,
and Melissa Lazarov

Design Coordinator:
Daniela Meda, Gabriele Nason

Editorial Coordinator:
Filomena Moscatelli

Proofreader:
Charles Gute

Copywriting and Press Office:
Silvia Palombi Arte&Mostre, Milano

US Editorial Director:
Francesca Sorace

Promotion and Web:
Monica D'Emidio

Distribution:
Antonia De Besi

Administration:
Grazia De Giosa

Warehouse and Outlet:
Roberto Curiale

This publication was conceived on the occasion of:

FRANCESCO VEZZOLI
Right You Are (If You Think You Are)
By Luigi Pirandello, 1917

October 27, 2007 at
Solomon R. Guggenheim Museum

Produced by
Gagosian Gallery
Performa 07
Solomon R. Guggenheim Museum

Photography on pages 21–25 and 72–73 by
Ashkan Sahihi; pages 26–27, 124, and back cover
by Matthias Vriens; pages 30–71 and 74–103 by
Jason Schmidt; page 123 by Rob McKeever and page
126–127 by Roberto Marossi.

We apologize if, due to reasons wholly beyond
our control, some of the photo sources have
not been listed.

Printed in January 2009
by Leva spa, Sesto San Giovanni
for Edizioni Charta

Edizioni Charta srl
Milano
via della Moscova, 27 - 20121
Tel. +39-026598098/026598200
Fax +39-026598577
e-mail: edcharta@tin.it

Charta Books Ltd.
New York City
Tribeca Office
Tel. +1-313-406-8468
e-mail: international@chartaartbooks.it
www.chartaartbooks.it

FRANCESCO VEZZOLI

RIGHT YOU ARE

(IF YOU THINK YOU ARE)

GAGOSIAN

CHARTA

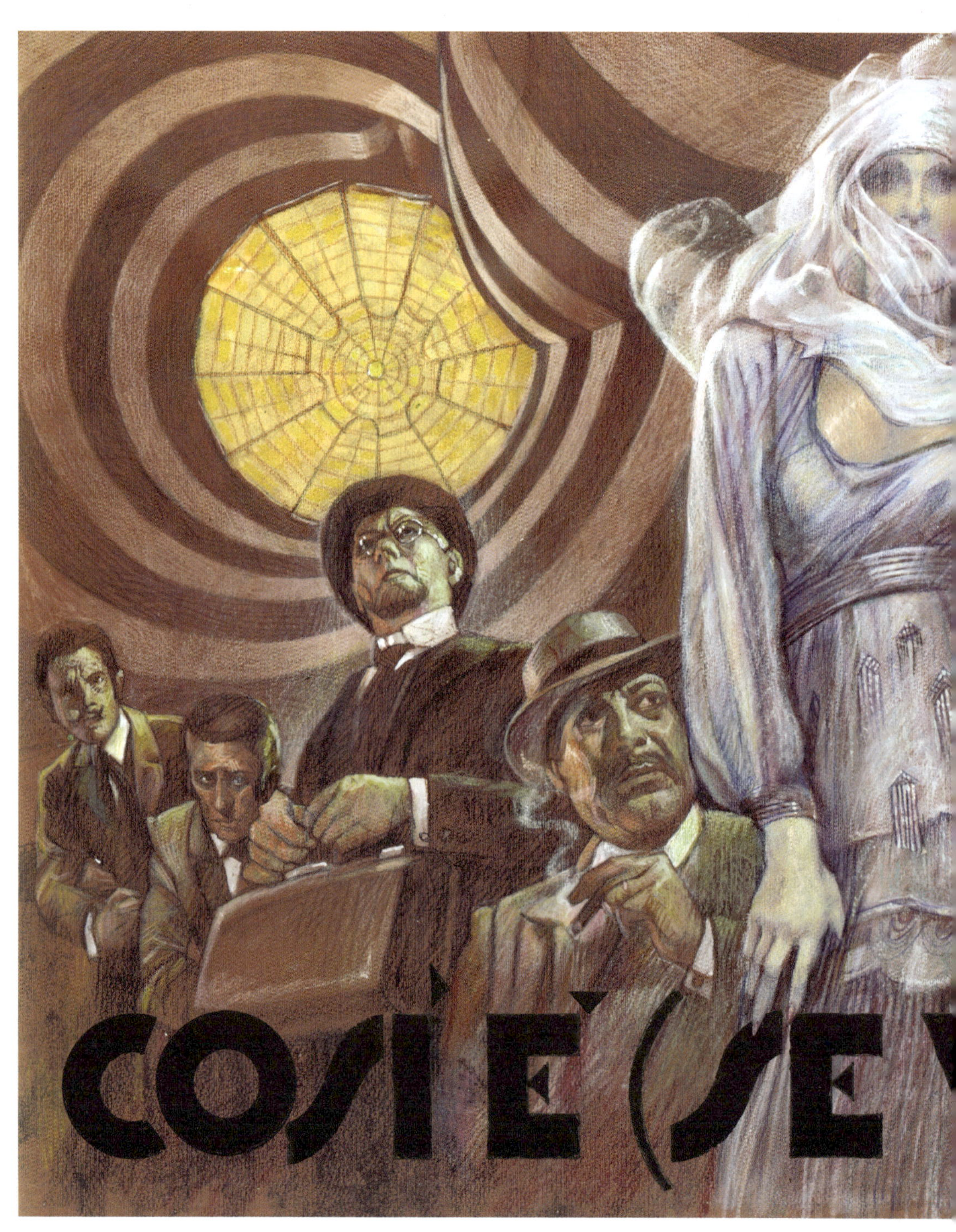

FRANCESCO VEZZOLI The Premiere of a Play That Will Never Run, 2007, Digital print on paper, unique, 52 ¾ x 71 inches, 134 x 180 cm. Design by Ermanno Iaia

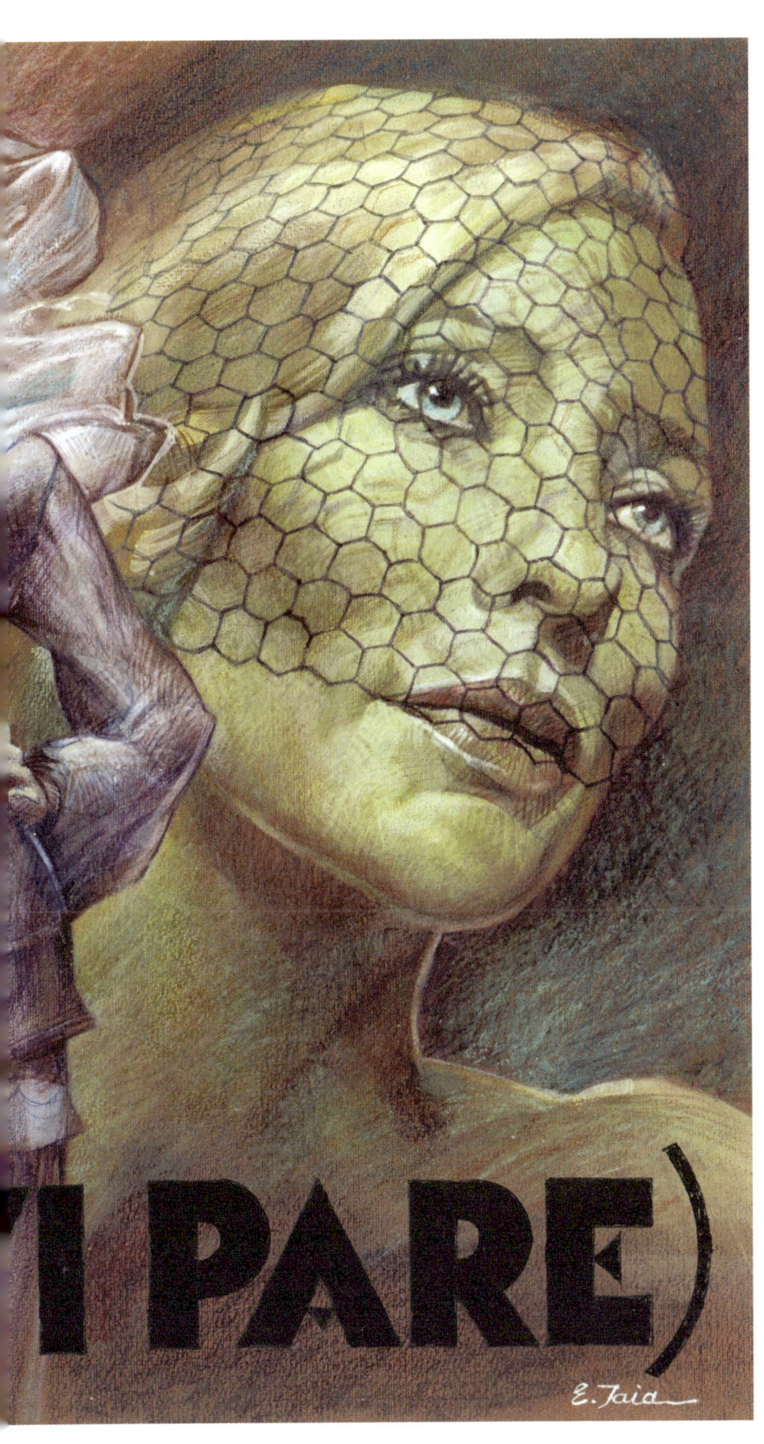
I PARE)

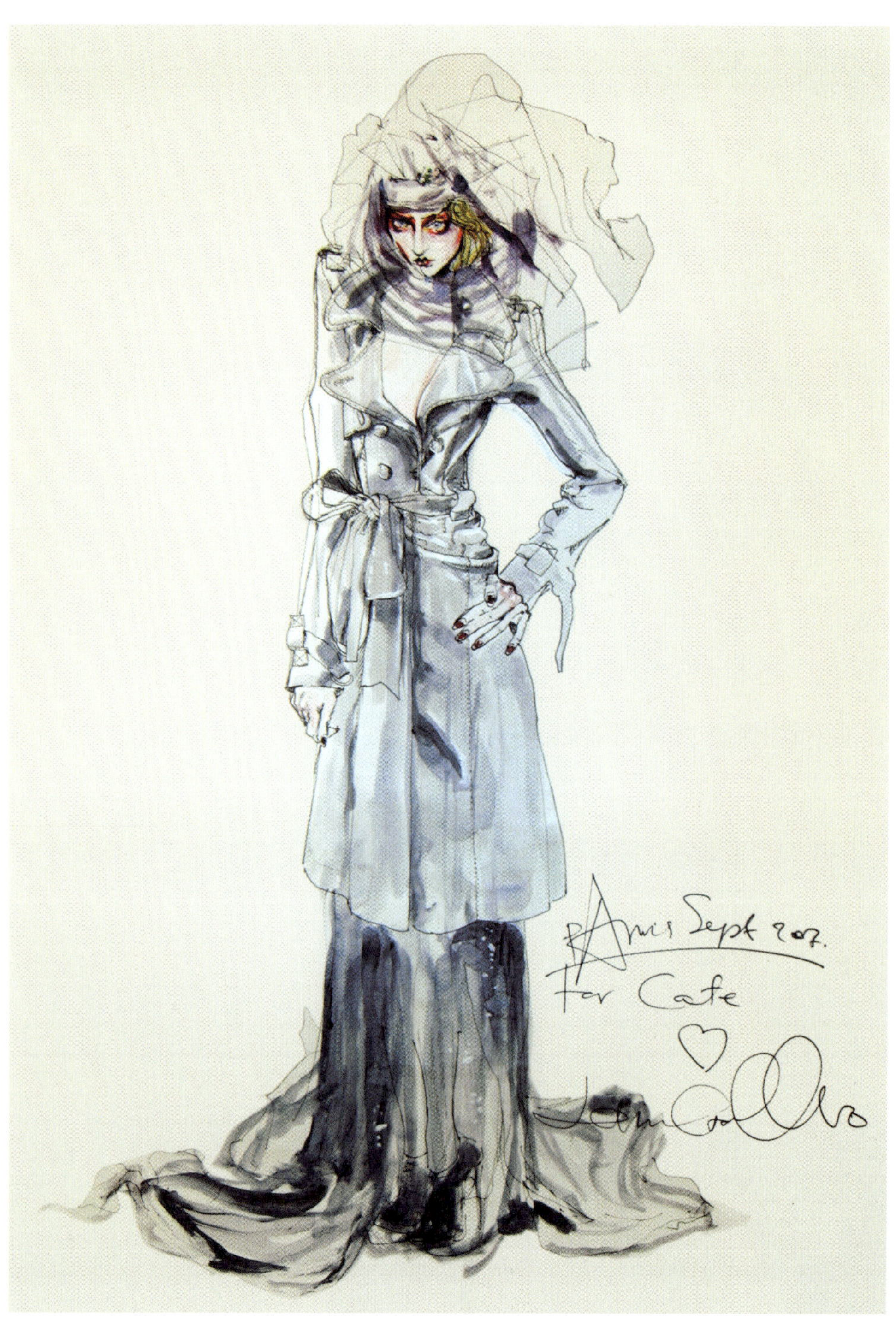

Costume design for Cate Blanchett by John Galliano for Christian Dior Couture

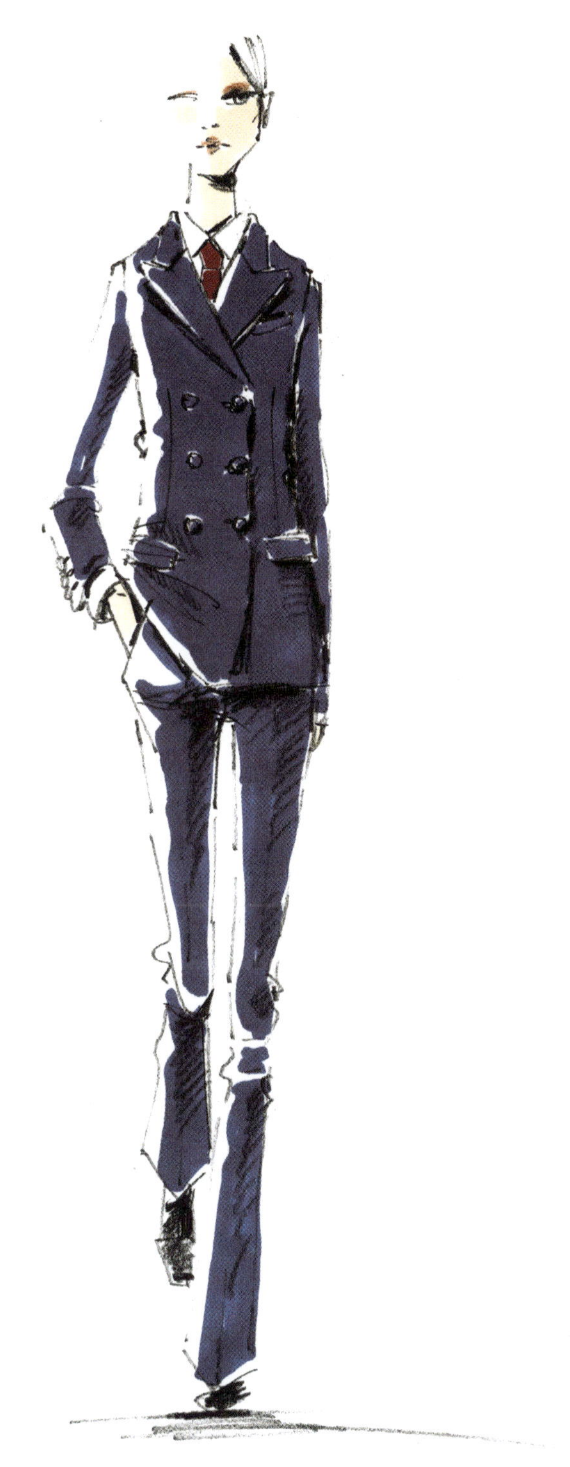

Costume design for Natalie Portman by Miuccia Prada

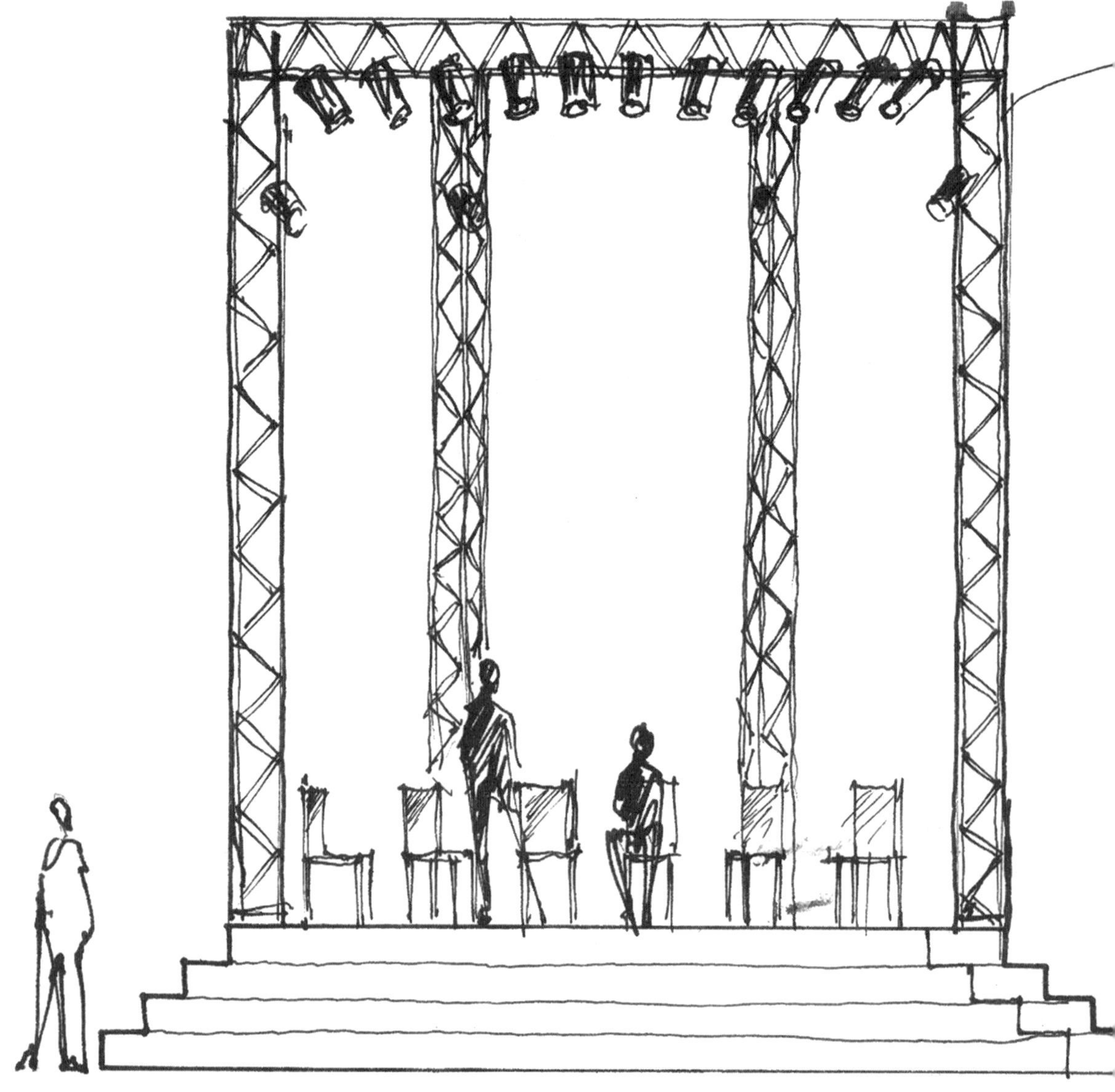

Stage drawings for <u>Right You Are (If You Think You Are)</u> by Scott Pask

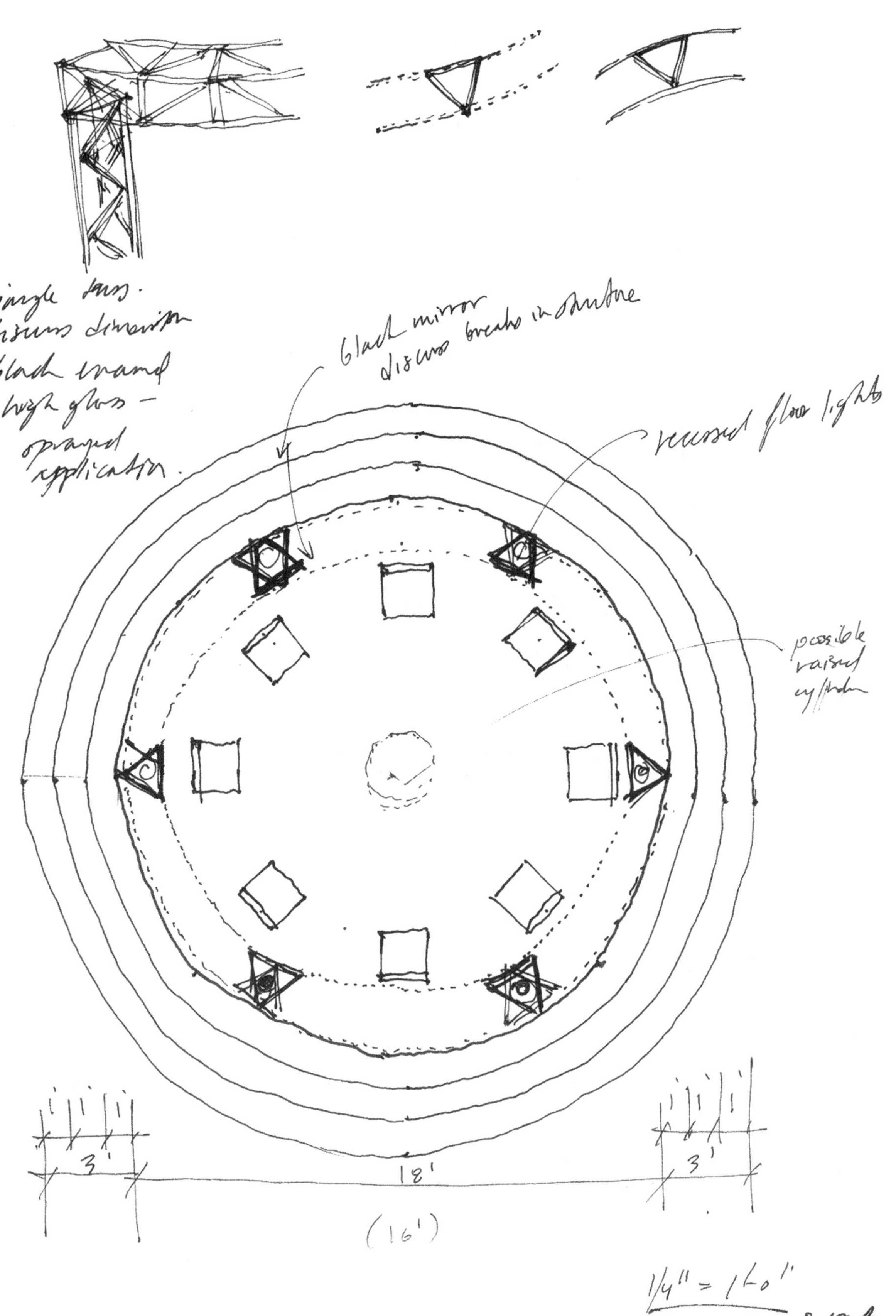

triangle truss.
discuss dimension
black enamel
high gloss —
sprayed
application.
black mirror
discuss breaks in structure
recessed floor lights
possible
raised
crystalu
18'
3'
3'
(16')
1/4" = 1'-0"
s. jordan

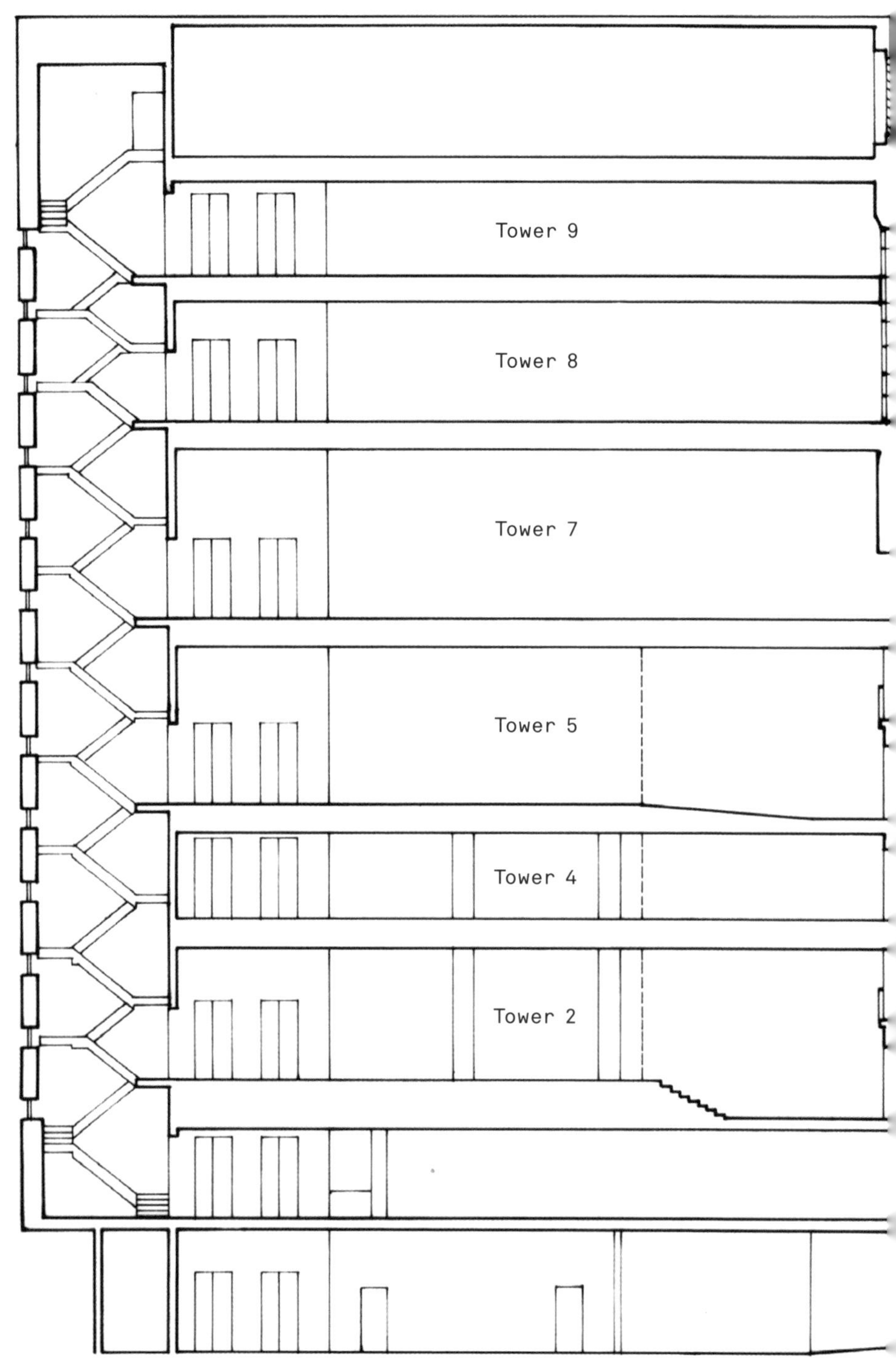

Solomon R. Guggenheim Museum elevation illustrating seating chart

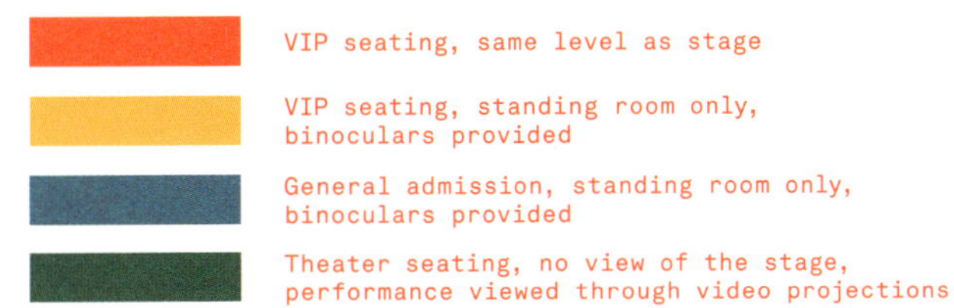

VIP seating, same level as stage
VIP seating, standing room only, binoculars provided
General admission, standing room only, binoculars provided
Theater seating, no view of the stage, performance viewed through video projections
Ramp 6
Ramp 5
Ramp 4
Ramp 3
Ramp 2
Ramp 1
Ground floor
Stage
Theater

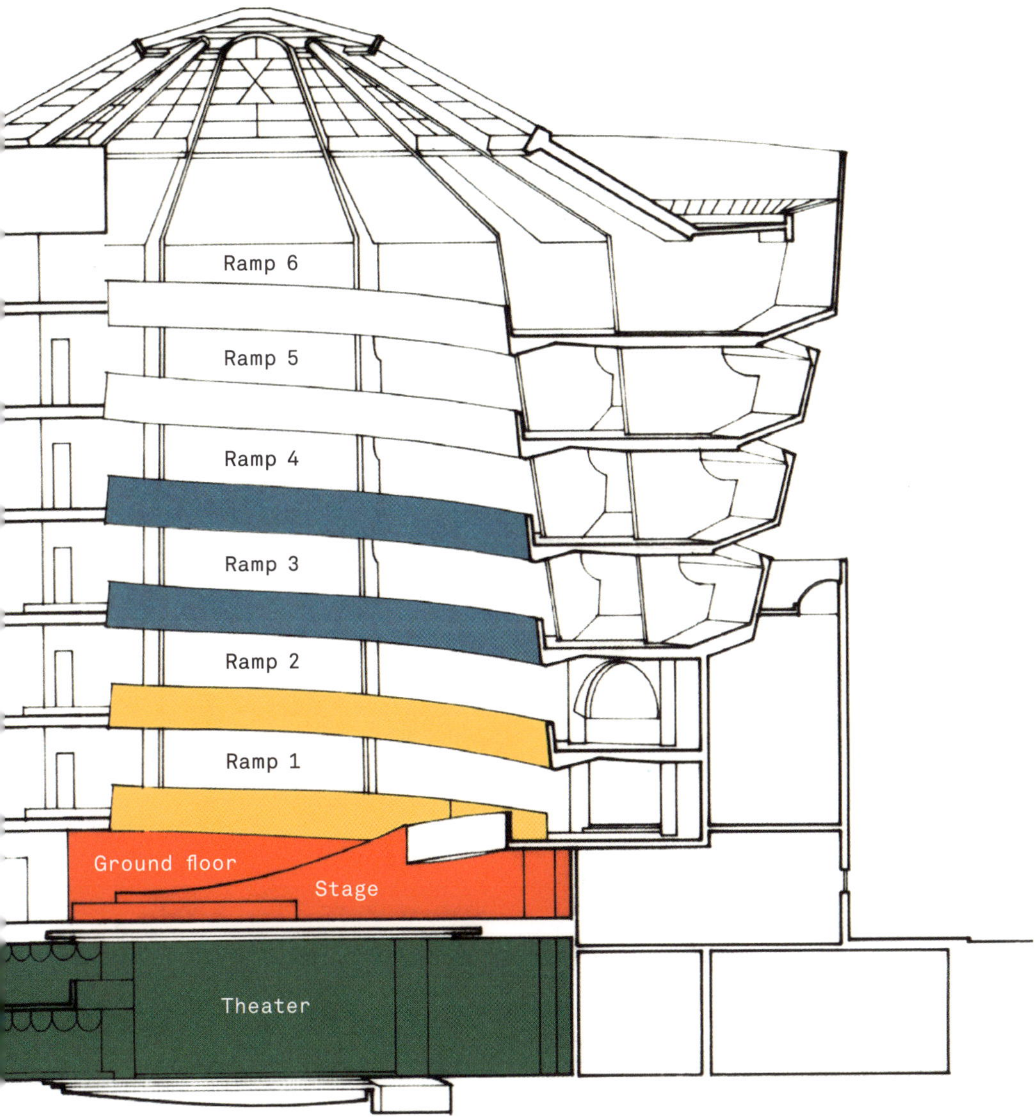

« PIRANDELLO! »

HERBERT MUSCHAMP

Relativity hit Pirandello pretty hard, wouldn't you say? Or perhaps it was really just the liquidation of Absolutism, or maybe the refusal of so many Absolutists to go away even though their day was done. You could point them toward a guttersnipe sniping in the gutter and tell them the pattern of snipes held the master key to all life's codes of meaning and value and they would be powerless to disbelieve you. So deeply engrained were the reflexes of belief in the existence of a single vantage point from which all meanings and values were identically perceived by all observers.

And if we will only do this, that, and the other thing, a minimum of five times a day, we will most definitely become known all across the land as The Keeper of the Key.

Who hasn't been "touched" by Relativity in this way? Who hasn't tried to earn the key to paradise? Only to discover that the combination to the lock is changed no fewer than ten times every 30.5 seconds? Or that the image of Paradise itself changes 196 times a minute? One nanosecond it will resemble Boboli Gardens. The next it will look like Lady Godiva. Then it will assume the gleaming form of a magical urn with silver spigots that gush steaming, dark hot chocolate into dainty porcelain cups.

This is to say that there is always a new audience out there looking for a Pirandello. The liquidation of the Absolute calls for a lyric poet. The Characters already found him in the last century. If it is taking a bit longer for fresh audiences to discover him, that's because there's a new one born every minute. A fresh crop of spectators is one of the greener forms Paradise takes. Is it holiday shopping time? Then a new group of souls must risk near drowning in a melted puddle where the North Pole once afforded a sturdy, level platform, with a single North Star hanging over the pole to light the one true way to Santa.

The poor slobs! For how can any of us avoid imagining that this terrifying sensation of meltdown is happening for the first time, ever, to anybody! From the impulse to relieve the panic, to convert, an audience is born. Its task is to convert the unfamiliar into patterns, dramas, crystals, rhymes, punch lines, hair-dos, Negative Capability, spaghetti with shaved white truffle.

And where formerly there was that single, unmoving North Star hanging in the heavens, there was now an endlessly changing cast of North Stars, sort of like the Latin boy group Menudo, in fact. Sort of like *you*, in fact, when the clock tower on the skyline of your city of subconscious fantasies announces that it's time for a make-over.

In the 1960s, Andy Warhol found a substitute for artistic content by asking viewers of his films to disbelieve in an inherent distinction between Hollywood movie stars and garden variety exhibitionists. This bright cheapskate maneuver coincided with the collapse of the studio system as a method for producing stardom; the rise of television as a primary source of family entertainment; and other assaults on the rickety pyramid of glamour. (The scrapping of transatlantic passenger ships was a blow from which that pyramid has never fully recovered, unless you can accept a piece of cloth sliding on a wire as a substitute for the stairway into a grand saloon lit by alabaster torchieres.)

Forty years later, Francesco Vezzoli began casting Jeanne Moreau, Catherine Deneuve, and other actors of bankably stellar renown in handmade art world artifacts. Short videotapes commissioned by galleries, museums, and private collectors, these products also reflected changing relationships between fine and popular art forms and the tensions such changes engendered. They reflected the era of the art star, a figure notably lacking a firm sense of separation from fame, luxury, and other worldly enticements. At the same time, Vezzoli's capacity to entice his roster of traditional movie talent called upon the Romantic view of art as a framework capable of lifting objects, people, and events to a transcendent space, above the purely material plane. But who says you can't have it both ways?

And why stop at two? What performer could work happily confined to such a limited repertoire? More to the point, what self could live contently while restricted to one or two moods, perspectives, roles in society, potential futures, temperaments, colorations, psychological contracts? No self could live that way, actually, certainly not in New York on the Fourth of July. Because a self that found itself with a good view of Macy's fireworks on the East River would very naturally want to model itself after those multiple report spectacles where three or four umbrella-shaped images succeed each other in the dark sky, the transitions between them presaged by shimmering clouds of gold and silver stars.

Now let's say you caught one of those whistling twizzlers. Would you expect it to be able to tell you which way is North? Of course not. But you could ask it to be the model for a personality that wants to project each of its facets into the dull night sky, one lying dormant within the fading shell of that preceeding, until all are tired and want to go home.

« FRANCESCO VEZZOLI'S PIRANDELLO: RIGHT YOU ARE! »

ROSELEE GOLDBERG

Luigi Pirandello, writing in June 1917 following the premiere of *Right You Are (If You Think You Are)* at the Olympia Theater in Milan, expressed his delight at how much he had annoyed the audience. "It has truly been a great success," he wrote to his sister Lina. "Not for the applause, but for the astonishment, the bafflement, the exasperation and the dismay I caused the audience. You don't know how much I enjoyed it!" His glee was not so different from that which F.T. Marinetti, poet, provocateur, and founder of the Futurists, had expressed in a manifesto for a new Futurist theater six years earlier. Take "pleasure in being booed," Marinetti instructed Futurist authors, believing that antagonizing an audience was the surest way to make them think, about the "monotonous procession" of their lives, for example, and also to pry them from a depressing "*passéist* theater," which he attacked for its "photographic reproductions of our daily life." Such desires to undermine audience expectations with surprises— "Sell the same ticket to ten people; traffic jam, bickering, and wrangling," Marinetti went so far as to suggest, or, "Offer free tickets to gentlemen or ladies who are notoriously unbalanced and likely to provoke uproars"—were part of the emotional matrix of Pirandello's writing as well, although his mischief was more cerebral and pressed into dialogue in which each word fought its opposite, showing the essential sameness of illusion and reality. Thus Pirandello hoped to force a wedge between the lie of theater and the truth of real life—or vice versa—in a play that examined how we come to know what we think we know—through rumor, hearsay, intuition, misunderstanding, and a hodgepodge of contradictory facts. Applied to the lives we live today, our obsession with celebrities and the marketplace of goods and services that they fuel, Francesco Vezzoli's staging of *Right You Are…* illustrated the sands on which identities are built; he could not have chosen a more appropriate Pirandello play for New York City or for our times.

That there was plenty of Futurist effrontery to go with it was part and parcel of an event constructed from scratch for one night only. The hour-long wait, as the temporary wiring and fixtures were installed, for a beautifully dressed crowd on Fifth Avenue outside the Guggenheim Museum, excitedly anticipating the big draw of major actors of stage and screen inside—Cate Blanchett, Ellen Burstyn, Anita Ekberg, Natalie Portman, Peter Sarsgaard, David Strathairn, Elaine Stritch, and Dianne Wiest—seemed further proof of the Futurist recipe for a "dynamic theater." "We believe that a thing is valuable to the extent that it is improvised (hours, minutes, seconds), not extensively prepared (months, years, centuries)," Marinetti and his cohorts wrote in the Futurist Synthetic Theater manifesto of 1915 and, indeed, this crowd of premier players, made up of authors, auteurs, and general aficionados from the worlds of art, dance, theater, music, fashion, film, and finance, improvised superbly their role as audience-in-waiting; some threw up their hands and stamped their feet dramatically, making a show of impatience as the hour dragged on; some maneuvered to the front of the line, hoping to be recognized by the gatekeepers and allowed into the museum before those behind them; others linked arms in the cold for warmth, or puffed on cigarettes. When the doors finally opened, the crowd surged into the vortex of the Guggenheim's central atrium, waving their color-coded tickets of yellow, green, and blue, only (for some) to be further annoyed when directed to the first, second, or third ramps, depending on the color of their ticket. This recalled the history of notoriously disgruntled audiences from performance history such as Picabia's *Rélache*, which apparently kept Picasso, Duchamp, and friends waiting on a freezing night outside the Théâtre du Champs Elysées, Paris, in 1924, and those who rioted on opening night at Stravinsky and Nijinski's *Rite of Spring* in the same theater a decade earlier.

The one hundred VIPs who received *red* tickets—among them Uma Thurman, Marian Goodman, Miuccia Prada, Lou Reed, Laurie Anderson, Salman Rushdie, Lucy Liu, Andre Leon Tally, and Maggie Gyllenhaal—were seated in the rotunda in a tight circle around a slightly elevated metal 'cage' that most closely resembled Bauhaus drawings of proscenium-less stages from the early 1920s. Walter Gropius's "Total-Theater," Farkas Molnar's "U-Theater," or Frederick Kiesler's "Space-Theater," which was built and put to use in 1924 in Vienna for a famous festival of theater and music (participants included Oskar Schlemmer, Ferdinand Leger, and Kurt Schwitters), could be thought of as axonometric precedents to this instant structure that cleverly provided a trestle for lighting fixtures, video cameras, and microphones inside an exhibition space not equipped with such basic theater tack. The actors sat on chairs in a circle facing each other, reading from scripts on music stands, paying close attention to their fellow performers while ignoring the audiences at their backs. Undistracted by the need for traditional acting techniques of emoting, projecting, or moving across a stage, each presented the self we all wanted to see most intently; the star in the flesh. With such limited action as turning the head to acknowledge a speaker, or using a hand to turn a page, the text was also secondary to the live presence of the well-known actors. Some of their words would be lost in the cavernous space, others at first came across as a babble of *non sequiturs*: "Who isn't interested in life? You are always so... Oh well, whatever, however. No, no—If I came in here and right in front of you, just right in front of you, worse actually..." says one of the characters early on, in typical Pirandello-speak. But eventually a story did add up, as the readers and the audience settled down, about the goings-on of a man, his wife, and his mother-in-law in a small town and their neighbors who watch and wonder about their behavior. As the group of eight people bicker amongst themselves, vying for points as to whose interpretation of the curious facts is the more precise or plausible, they return, as though in refrain, to Pirandello's basic adage: "We are—all of us—many things to many people. So, who can finally say what is true?"

This spare reading in the hands of experienced and accomplished performers became a laboratory of sorts for watching closely how actors work; how each approaches a text for the first (or perhaps second or third) time and coaxes meaning from it while taking the measure of the play's pacing from the ensemble as a group. *Right You Are...,* as seen at the Guggenheim Museum, was a drawing, a sketch, a draft illustrated by live actors, yet one whose concentrated focus nevertheless gave a strong sense of Pirandello's ironic filter—and Vezzoli's as well. Both Italians have equal parts irony and humor in their bones that is essential *commedia del'arte.* Both revel in the theatricality of everyday life—"everything of any value is theatrical" is a line from another Futurist manifesto—and both make little separation between the two. Because both playwright and artist tend to build their work on concepts rather than narratives, there was no need for Vezzoli to indicate a particular time or place for the action. Neither a period piece nor a reconstruction in any way, the work instead exuded a present-day aesthetic and, in Vezzoli's hands, a high-end, seductive one as well. For Vezzoli revels in the exhilaration of movie-stardom magic. He lives on a plane where the drive of his imagination is always at full throttle and where stylized enticement and the pleasures it sets in motion is material for his art. As such he can steal imagery at will from his various heroes—Gore Vidal and Frederico Fellini among them, who represent for him untrammeled desire—and no doubt with their blessing, were he to ask for it, since his artistic framing devices re-animate and extend the lives of these maestros' own visionary obsessions. To place Anita Ekberg on Salvador Dalí's bright pink Mae West sofa, atop the covered fountain to one side of the Guggenheim's rotunda (of course a reference to the magnificent Trevi fountain of *La Dolce Vita*) to "look down on the Dolce Vita of New York" as Vezzoli explained, was the equivalent of the artist raising a glorious monument to the "unforgettable, long-lost historic moment" of 1960s cinema and the unimaginable levels of craving that it induced. "My Surrealist Queen," as Vezzoli calls Ekberg, "represents timeless beauty, [she] embodies the desire of more than one generation; she is the living memory" of a period that he resuscitates in order to examine in detail the powerful imaginative forces that made it work. That so many top-tier actors agreed to join him in this venture is a measure of their own interest in grasping what it is that they themselves love most dearly about their art, and the parts that they don't, in particular the blanket of public awareness that settles over them with their successes, as well as their respect for an artist from a different field who derives his content from their own.

Reflecting on the nature of performance, the elements of theater, and the drama of spectacle, *Right You Are…* was the work of a visual artist, not a theater director or dramaturge, who would be more intent on representation and meaning and in communicating ideas to an audience in a less circuitous way. Instead, Vezzoli chose to activate the space by filling it from top to bottom with the living characters that constitute the cultural and entrepreneurial worlds of the modern metropolis. Performers and audience both served his ends equally as instruments to activate an installation on the scale of an entire building; no single view or perspective dominated another, and all elements were consciously utilized, from the street outside to the cupola inside, including the elevator and the theater below ground, where a second parallel play, a live feed of the action from the rotunda of the museum, was taking place before a rapt audience. There, in the intimate comfort of a small theater, with unobstructed views and the benefit of hi-tech audio amplification, those who thought they had been relegated to the 'overspill' discovered that they had possibly the best seats in the house. On a large screen, close-ups from eight cameras showed alternating headshots of each actor as she or he spoke, the front row of the audience in the rotunda, and a bird's-eye view of the inverted ziggurat of the building's distinctive core. A vivid patchwork of screens, resembling the editing room of a TV studio during a ballgame, combined to create an exciting situation theater that was both live and mediated at the same time. The result was from the brightly lit podium and meandering audience members upstairs; downstairs the actors were reinstated in their more familiar medium of film, and were all the more comprehensible and accessible for it. The downstairs crowd also had the unexpected pleasure throughout of the company of actress Cate Blanchett, who, in Dior gown and veiled hat, sat straight-backed on a bench to one side, watching the action on screen. Shortly before the end of the evening, she made her way from the theater, via elevator, to the fourth floor to begin her grand, flurried descent, to a soundtrack of thunder and lightning. The statuesque Blanchett, in her role as the elusive Signora Ponza, stepped into a halo of lights trained on the stage, and, with arms raised, and in a booming voice, declared the infamous final words of Pirandello's play, satisfying at last, the long wait of the night with her existential haiku: "I am neither, I am either, I am no one, I am anyone. I am whoever you believe me to be."

That Vezzoli's performance was an unequivocal response to the architectural theatricality of Frank Lloyd Wright's masterpiece was also its essential *raison d'etre*. Inspired by a history of events that have animated the Guggenheim's interior since the building's inception in 1959—including performances by Meredith Monk, Vanessa Beecroft, Matthew Barney, and most recently Marina Abramović—Vezzoli chose to create his first live performance in this unorthodox space precisely to exploit its unusual vistas and concentrated energy. His work of many parts meshed in such a way as to make it seem that the notoriously difficult exhibition space, with its spiraling ramps that give the sensation of perpetual motion, was conceived by the architect from the start as a place for public assembly and imaginative drama. Vezzoli's *Right You Are…* was an evocation of the very nature of theater, its language, physicality, and conceptual richness, including the passions, conceits, and desires of its audience. It also fulfilled Vezzoli's plan, which he expressed in our very first meeting when he accepted our invitation to create a Performa Commission: "As *Caligula* is to Hollywood," he began, referring to his earlier film, "So Pirandello is to Performa. I have the perfect piece for you." And so it was.

Celebrities and crowd

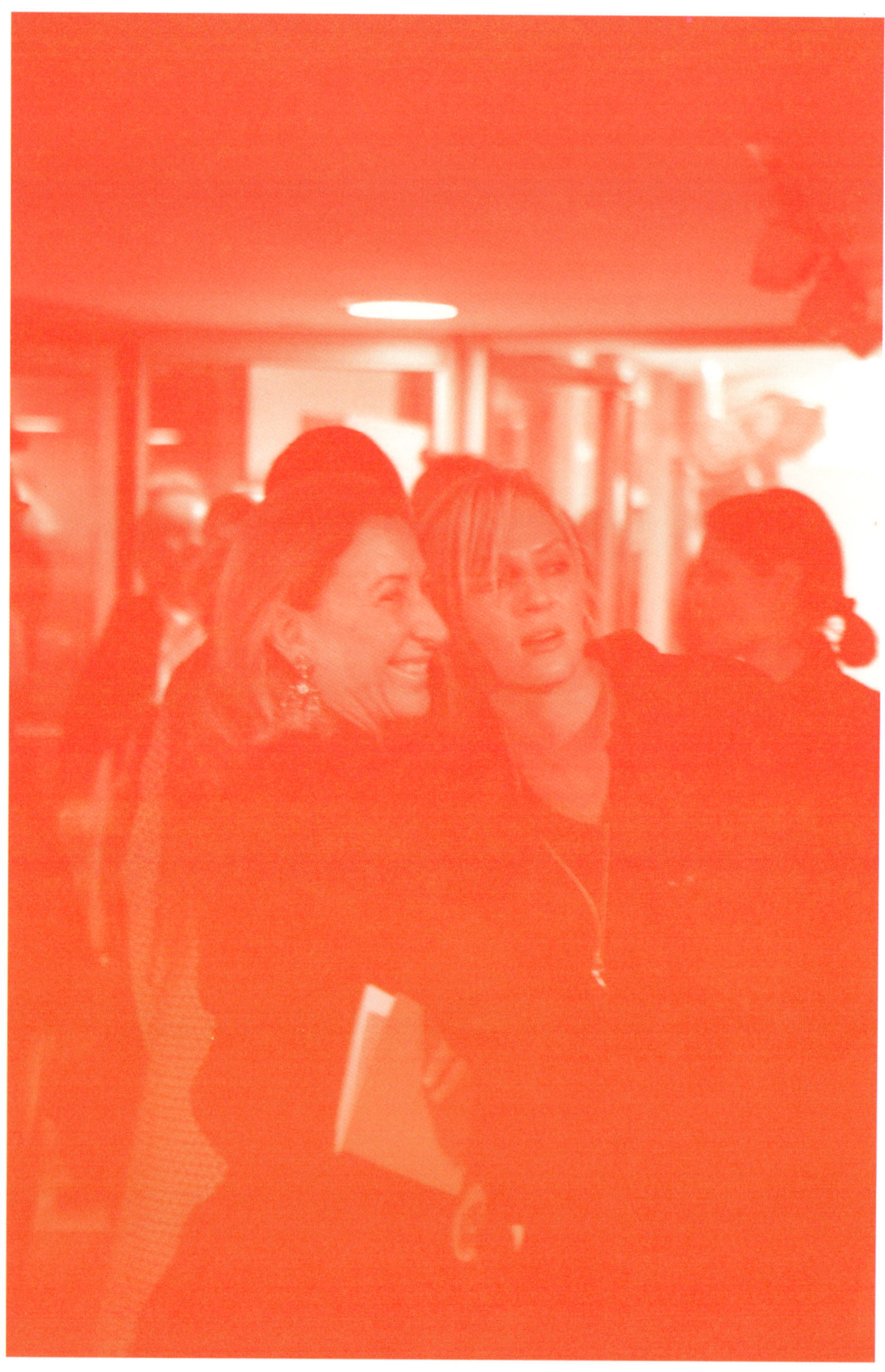

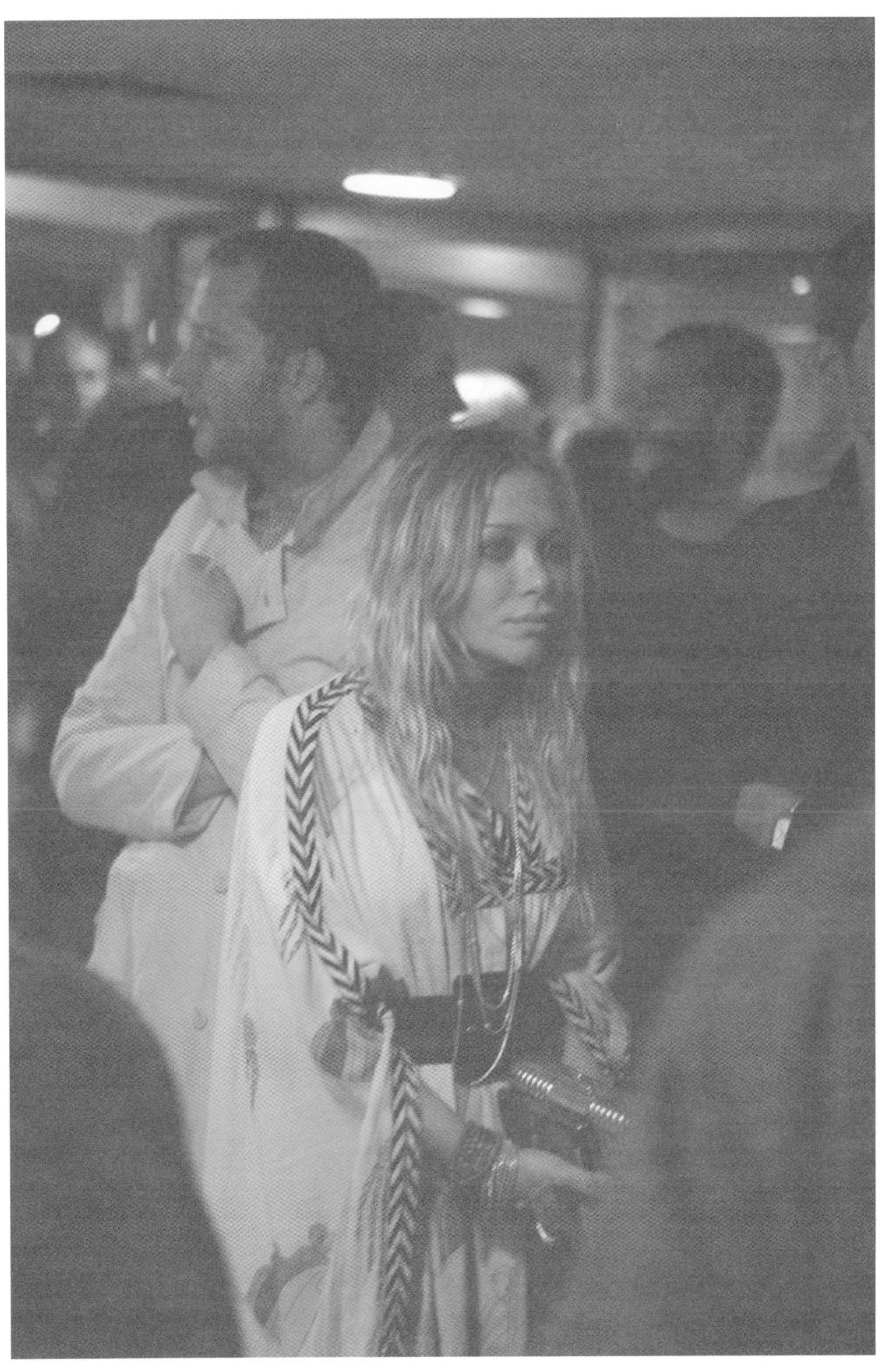

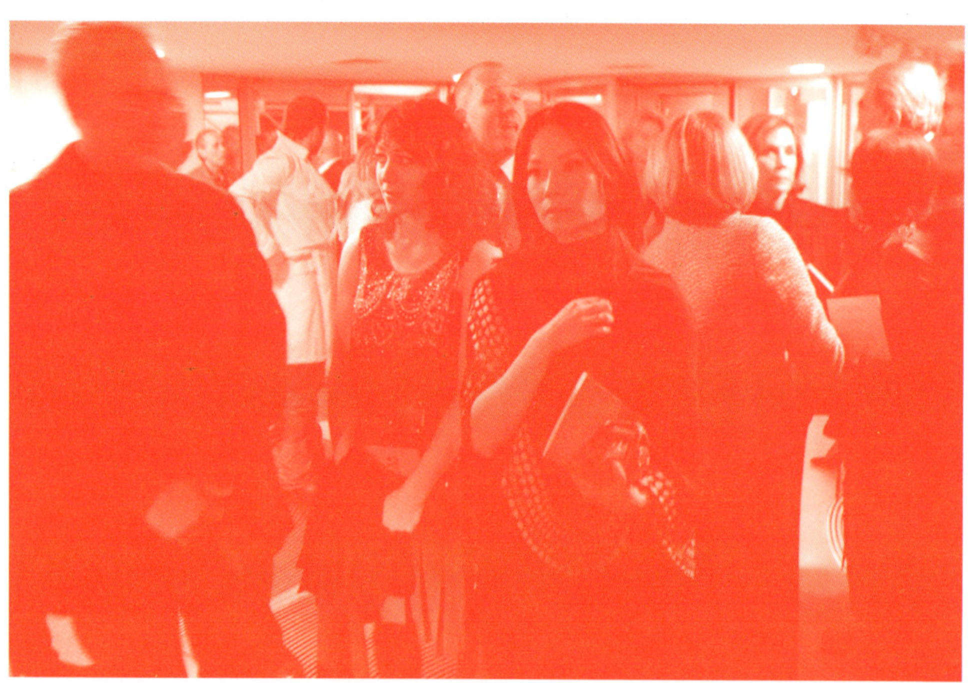

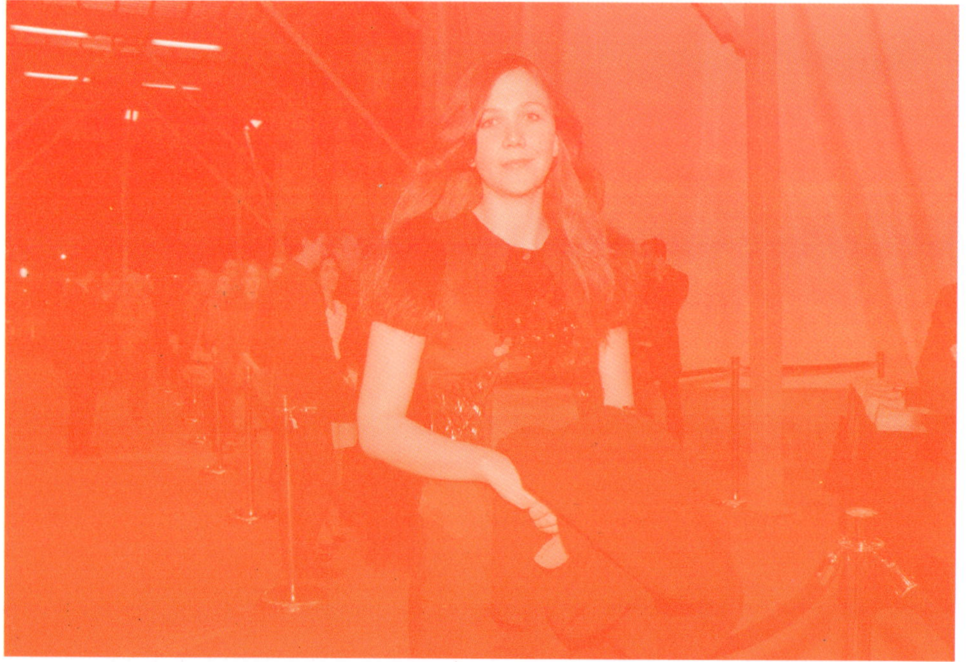

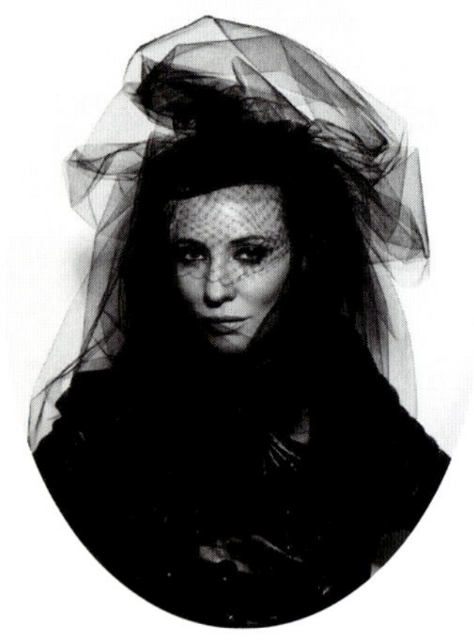

CATE BLANCHETT
SIGNORA PONZA

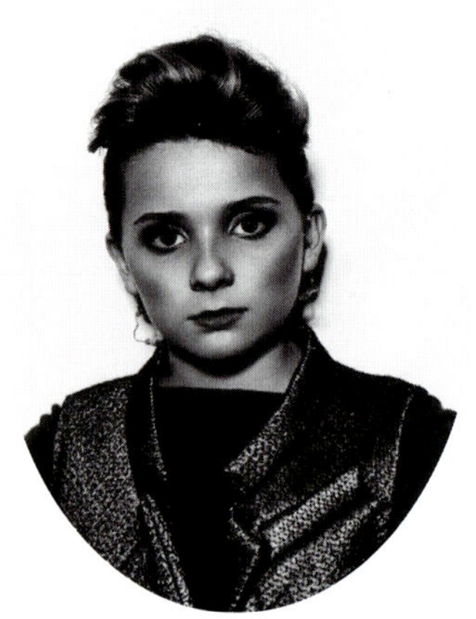

ABIGAIL BRESLIN
DINA

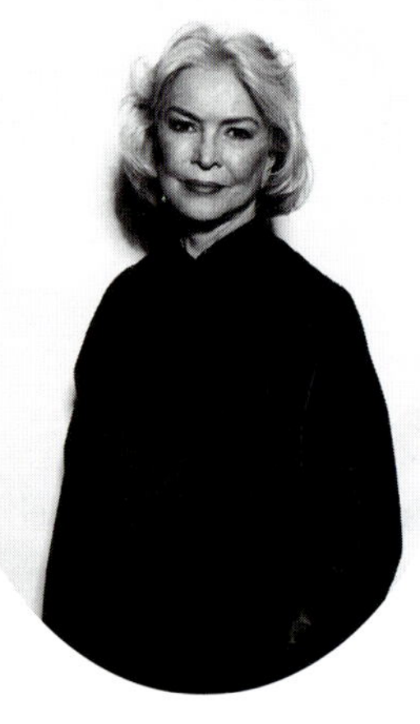

ELLEN BURSTYN
SIGNORA FROLA

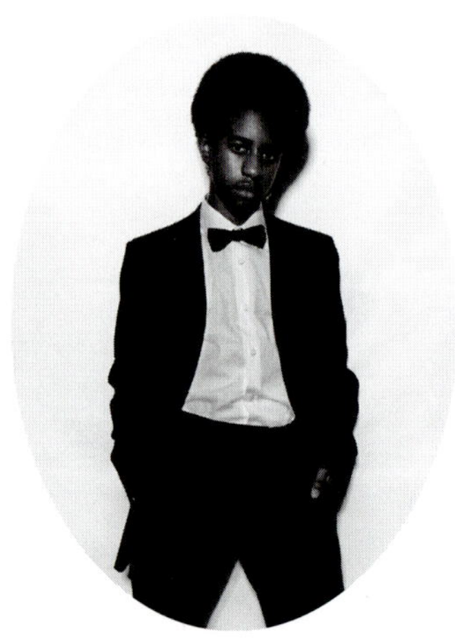

MARCUS CARL FRANKLIN
ANNOUNCER/MAYOR

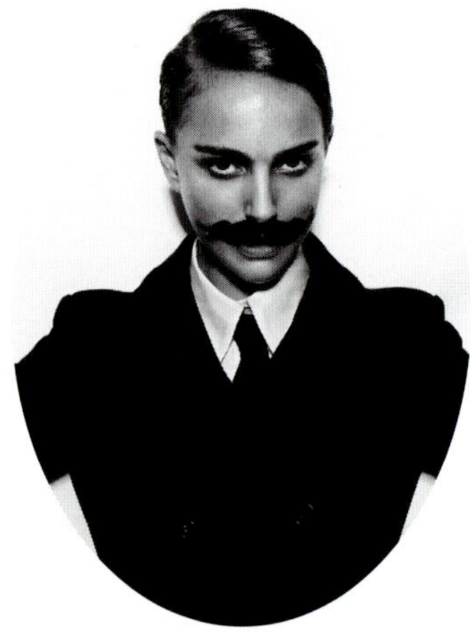

NATALIE PORTMAN
LAUDISI

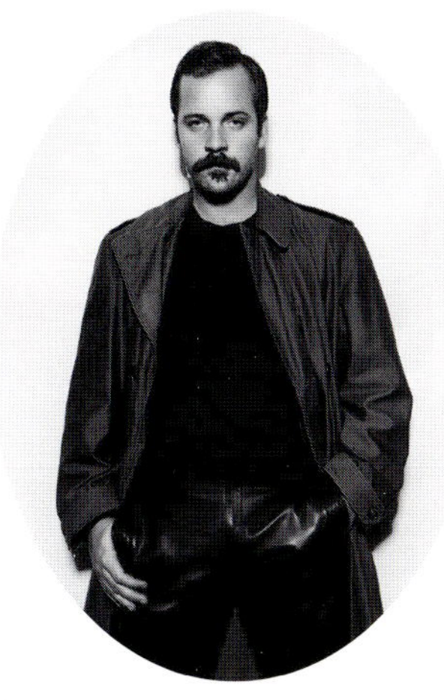

PETER SARSGAARD
AGAZZI

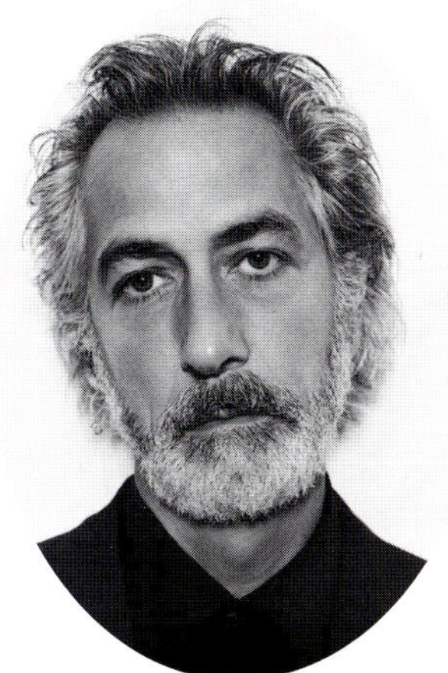

DAVID STRATHAIRN
SIGNOR PONZA

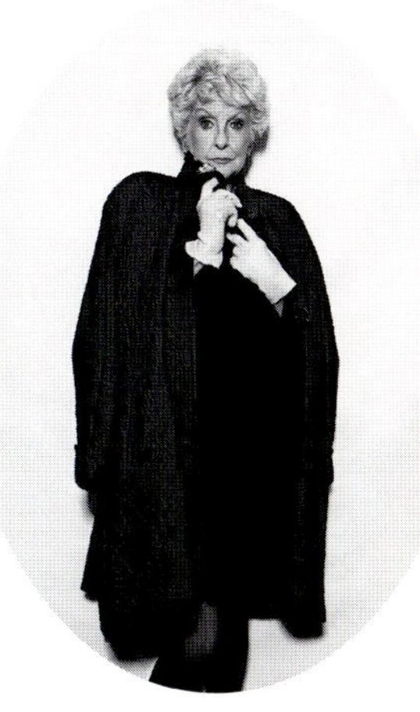

ELAINE STRITCH
SIGNORA CINI

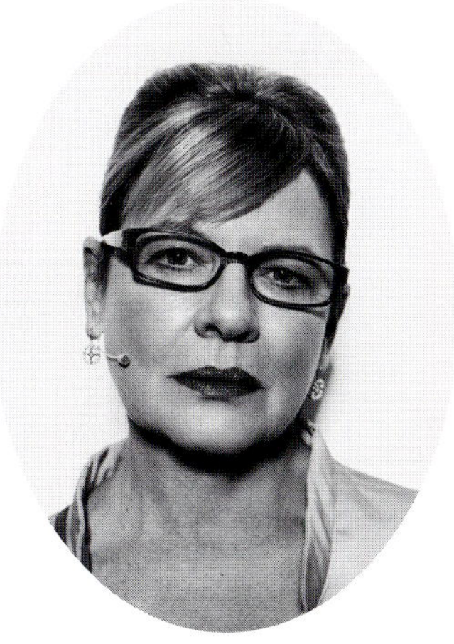

DIANNE WIEST
AMALIA AGAZZI

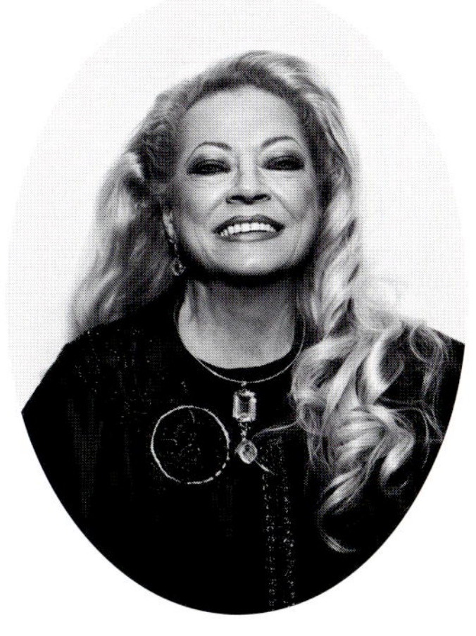

ANITA EKBERG

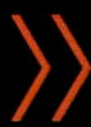

WE ARE—ALL OF US
—MANY THINGS TO
MANY PEOPLE. SO,
WHO CAN FINALLY SAY
WHAT IS TRUE?

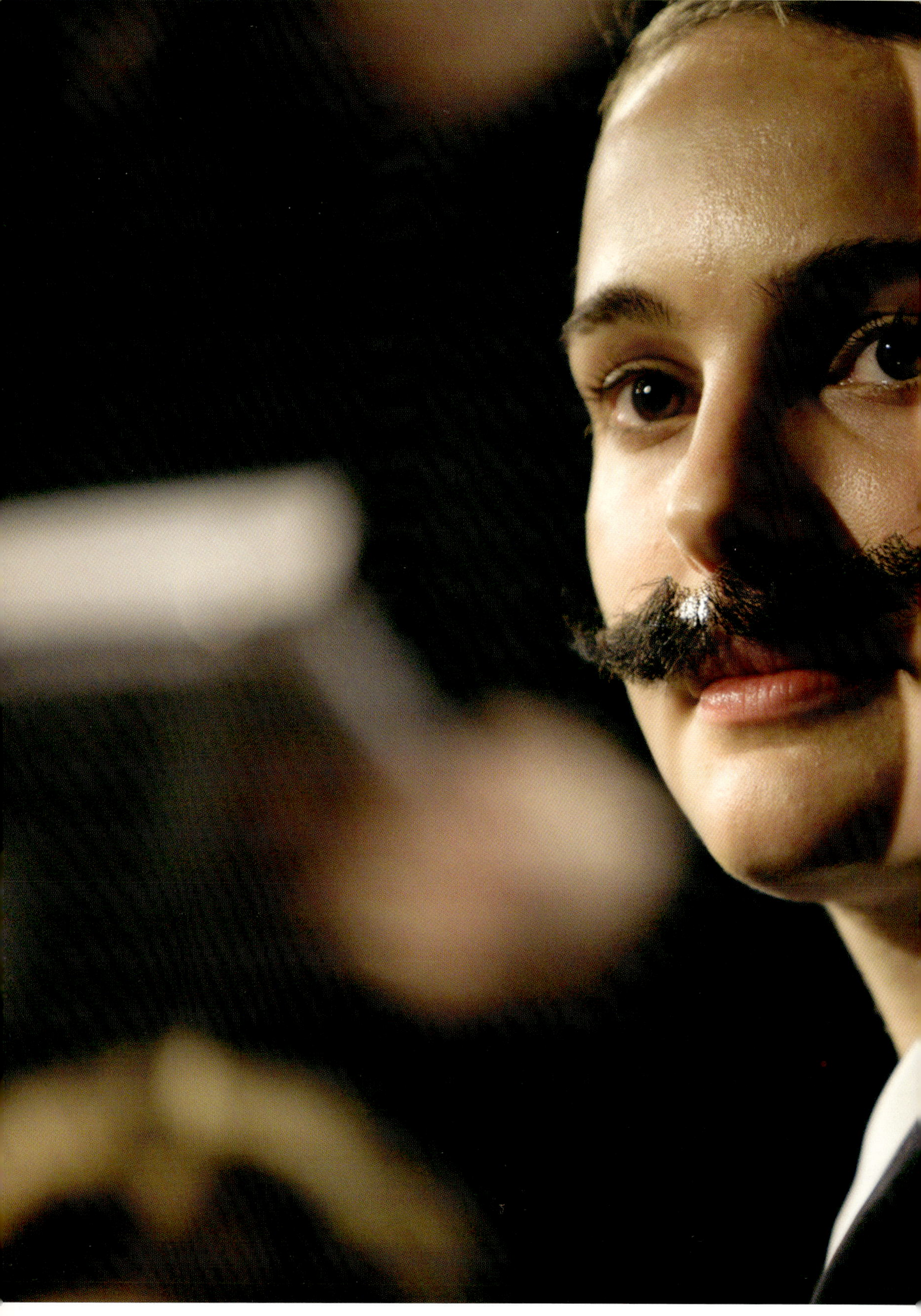

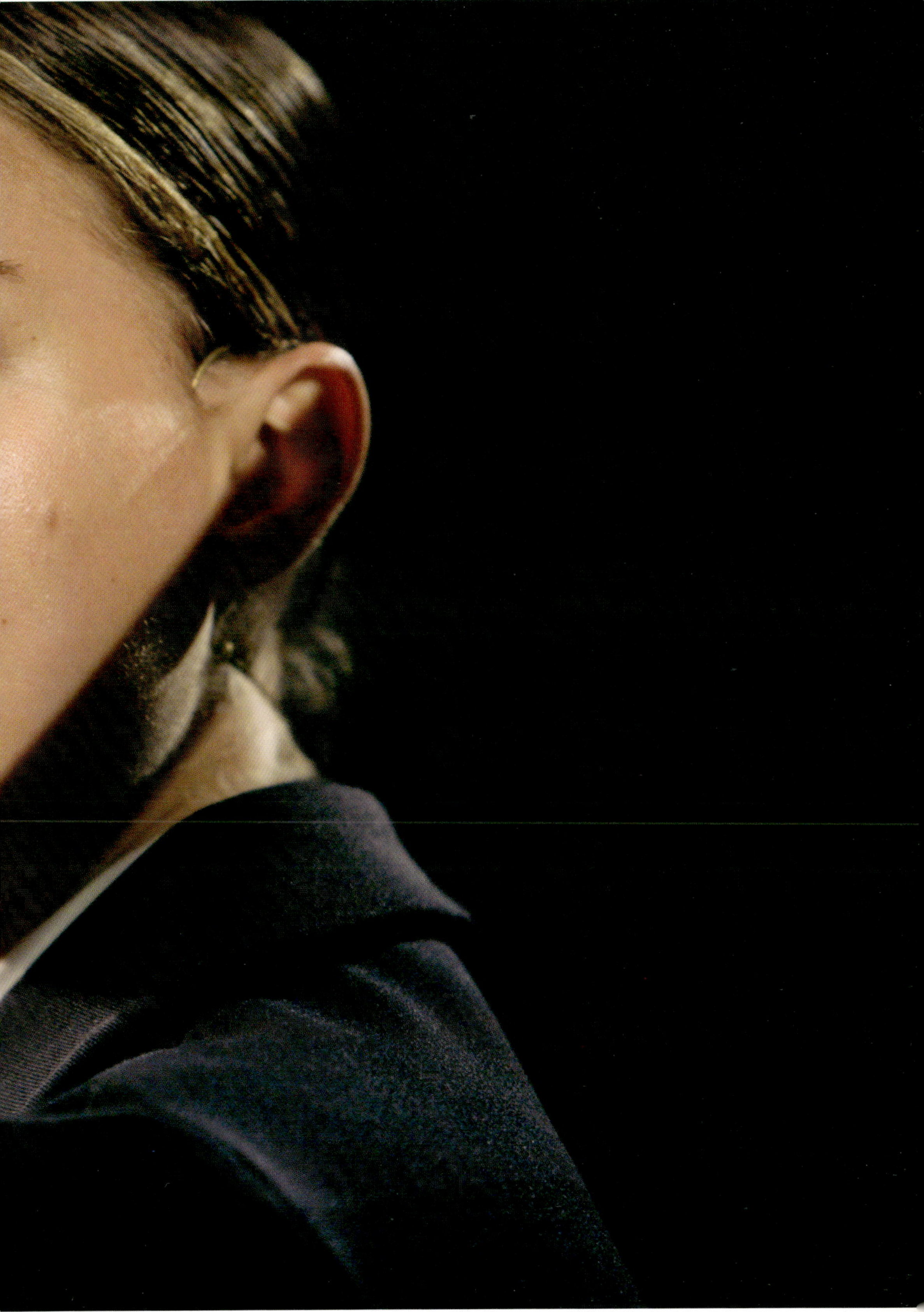

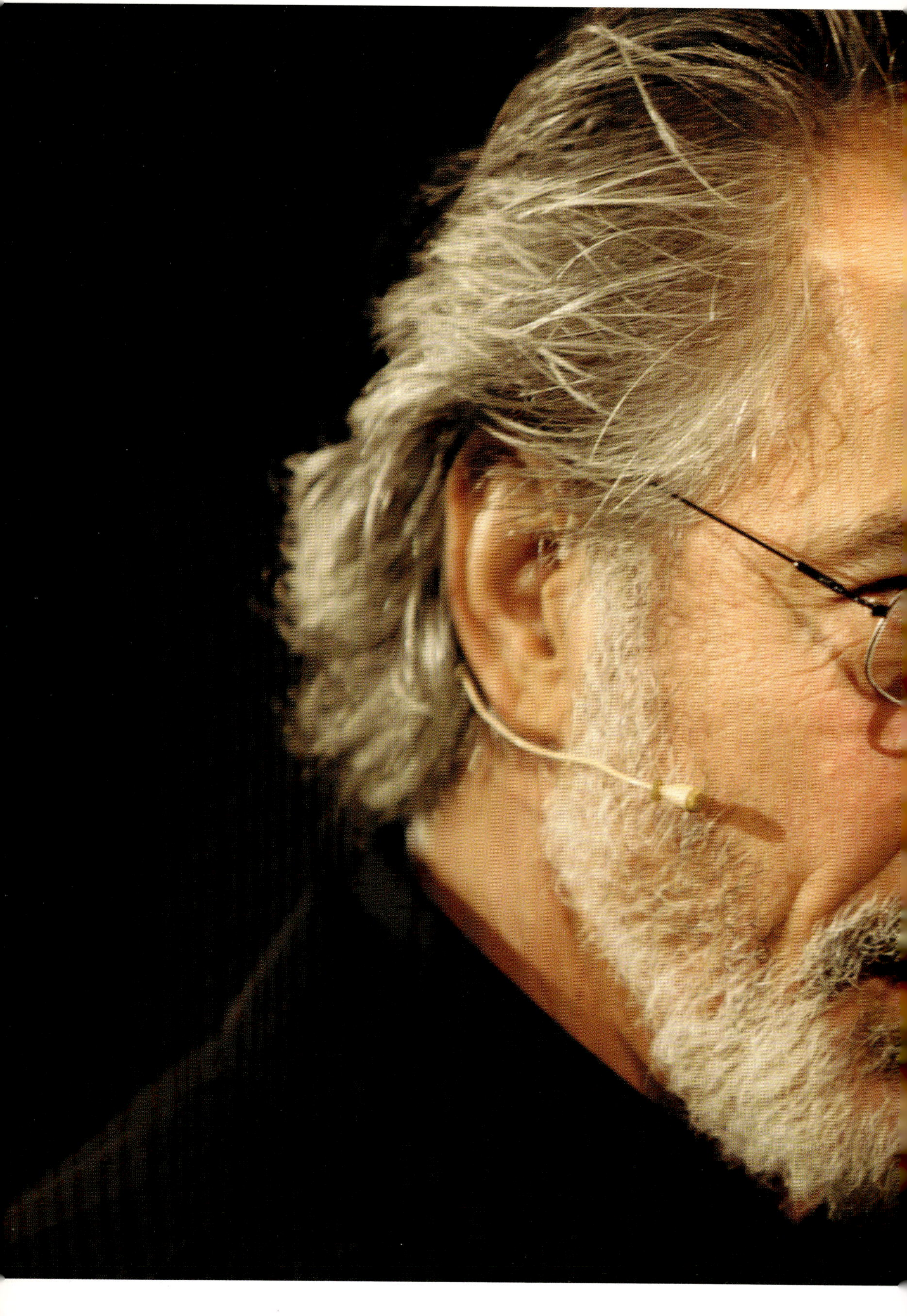

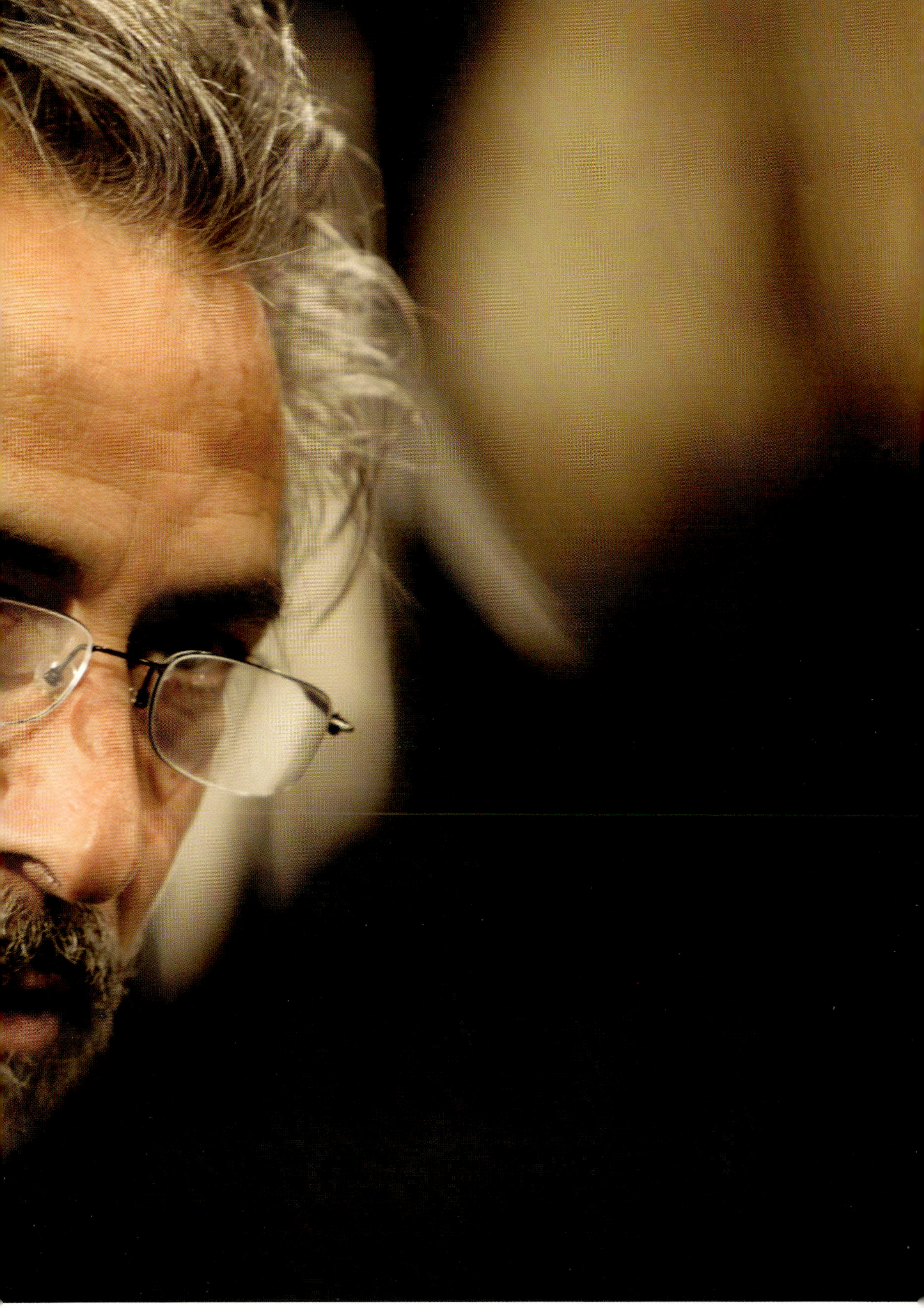

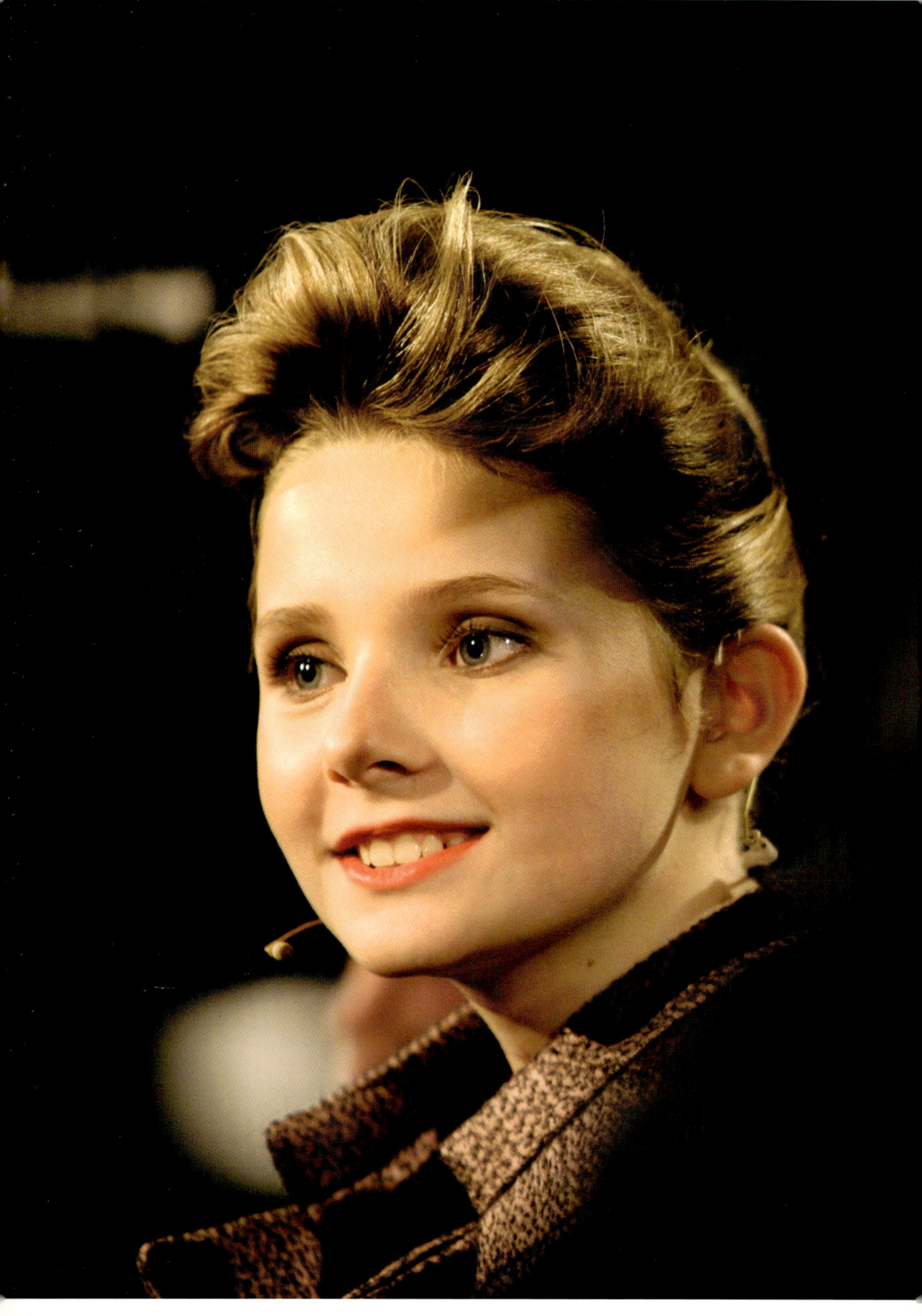

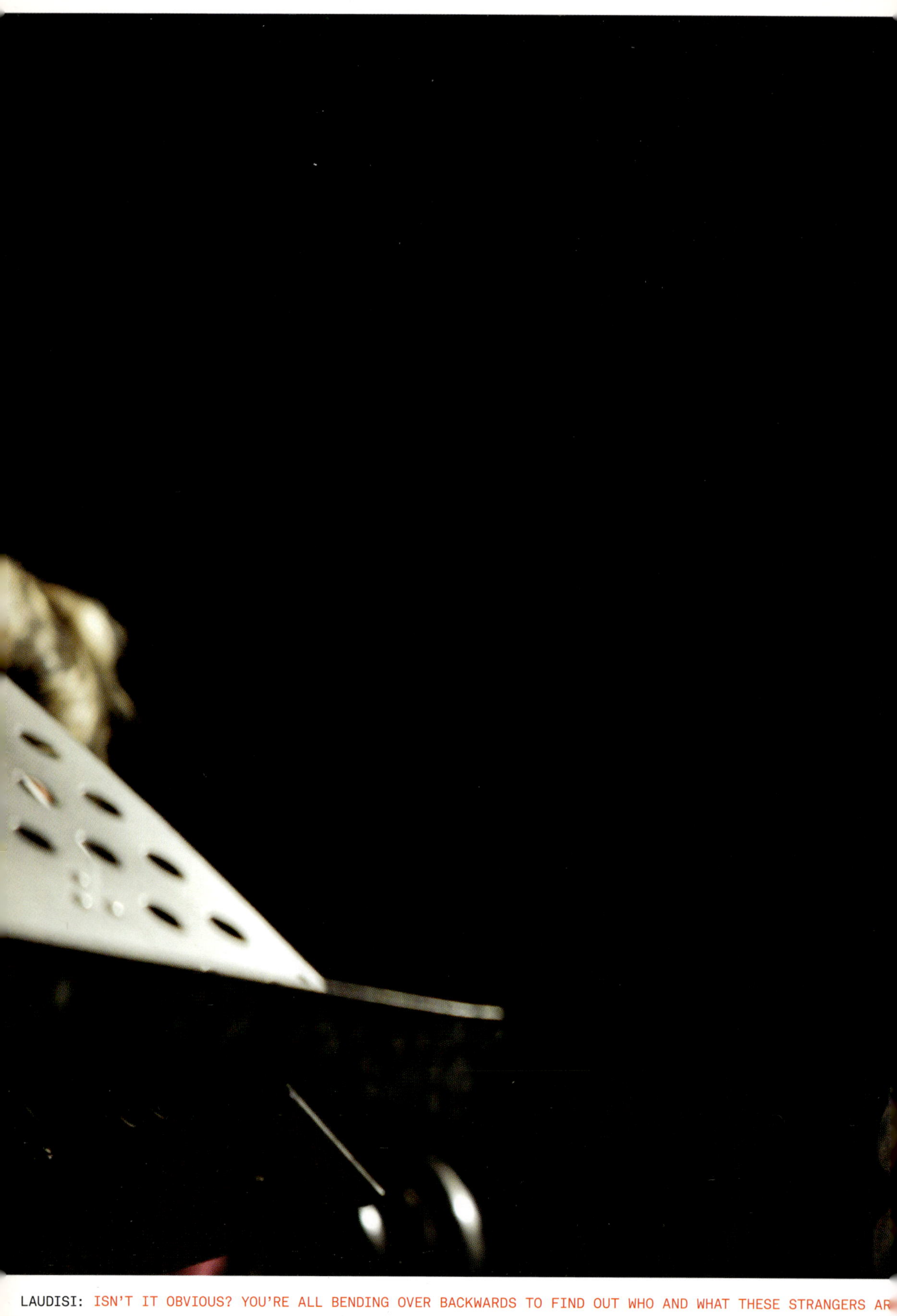

LAUDISI: ISN'T IT OBVIOUS? YOU'RE ALL BENDING OVER BACKWARDS TO FIND OUT WHO AND WHAT THESE STRANGERS AR

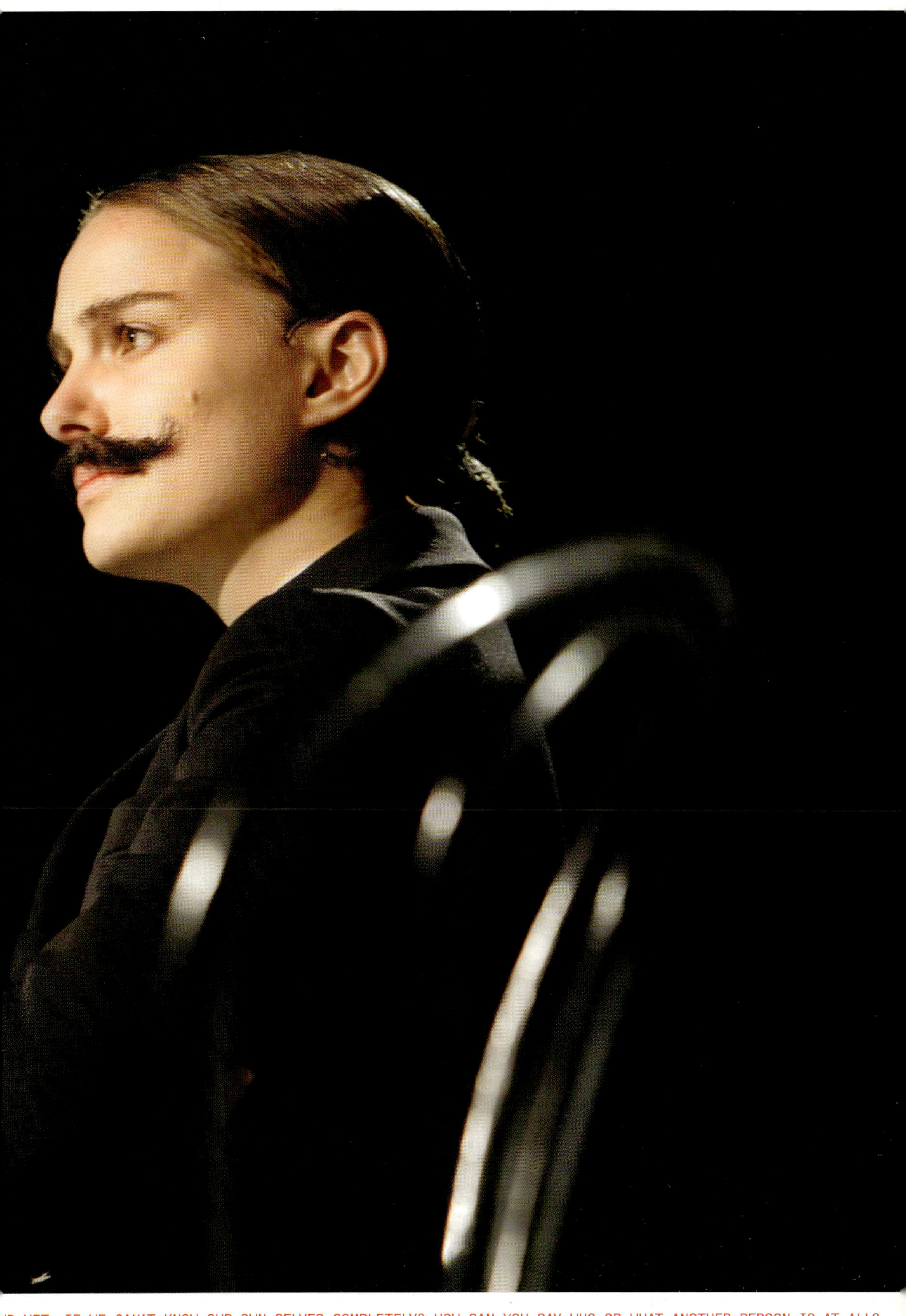

ND YET, IF WE CAN'T KNOW OUR OWN SELVES COMPLETELY? HOW CAN YOU SAY WHO OR WHAT ANOTHER PERSON IS AT ALL?

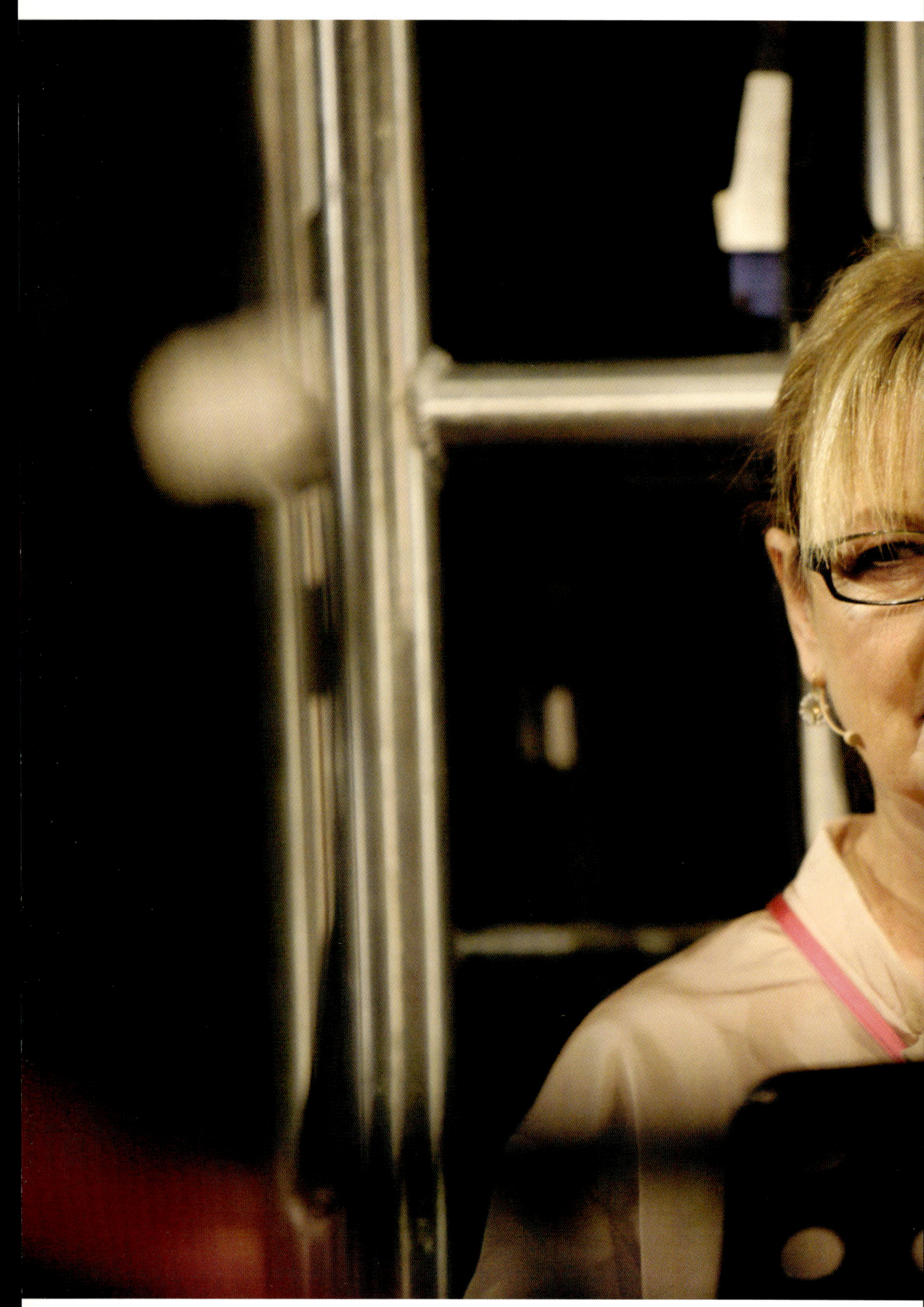

AMALIA AGAZZI: SO THE TRUTH IS IMPOSSIBLE? HEAVEN HELP US.

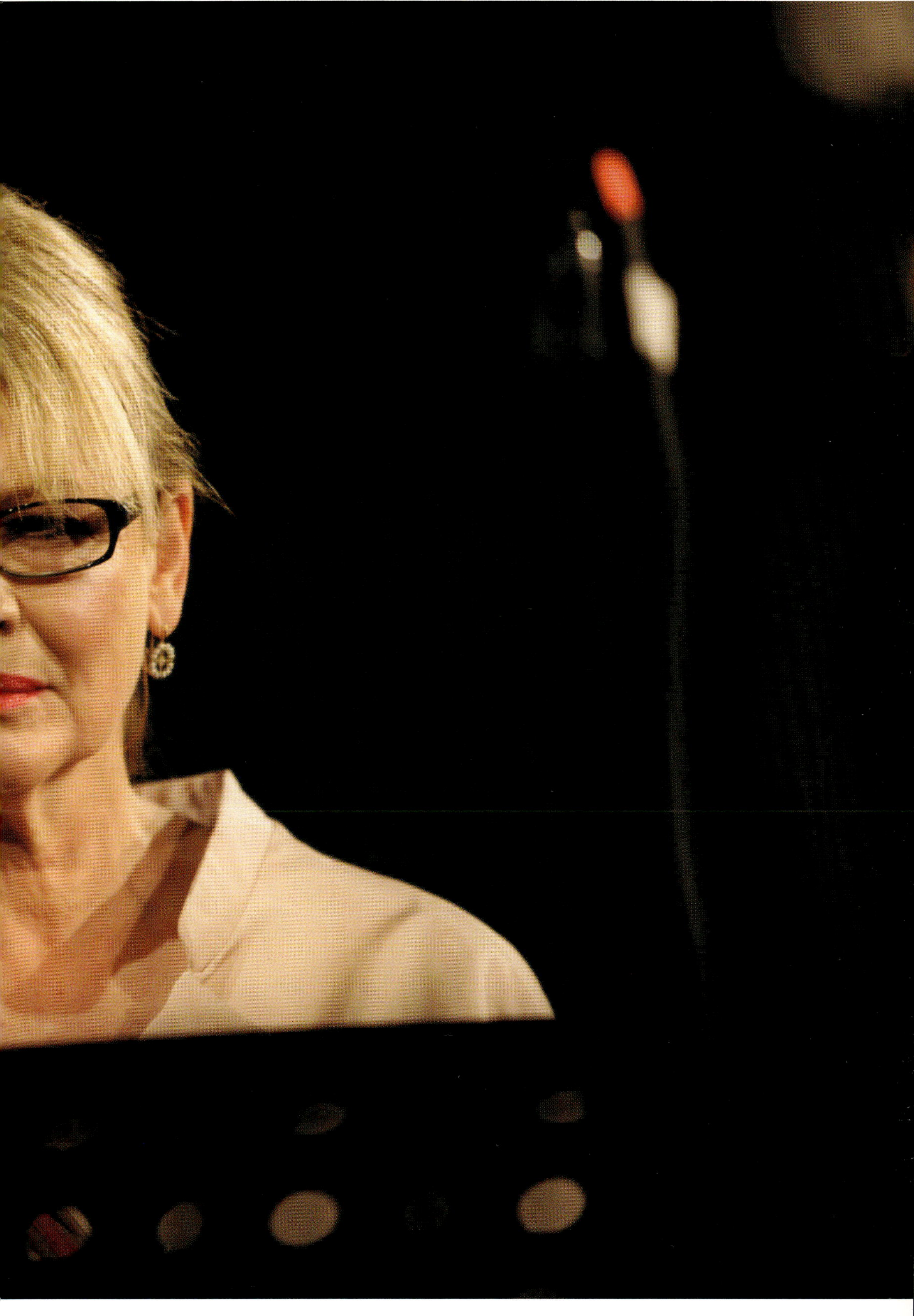

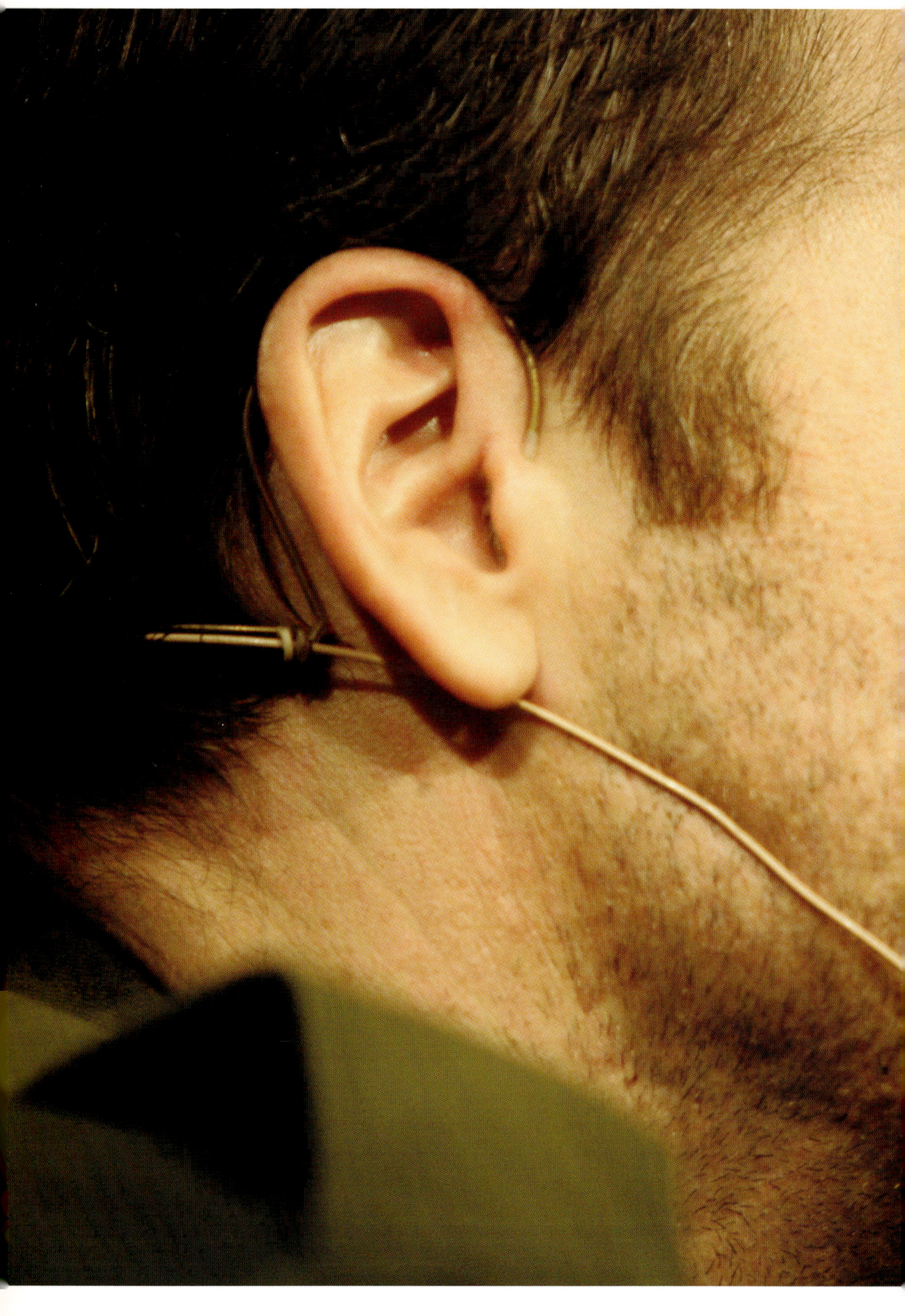

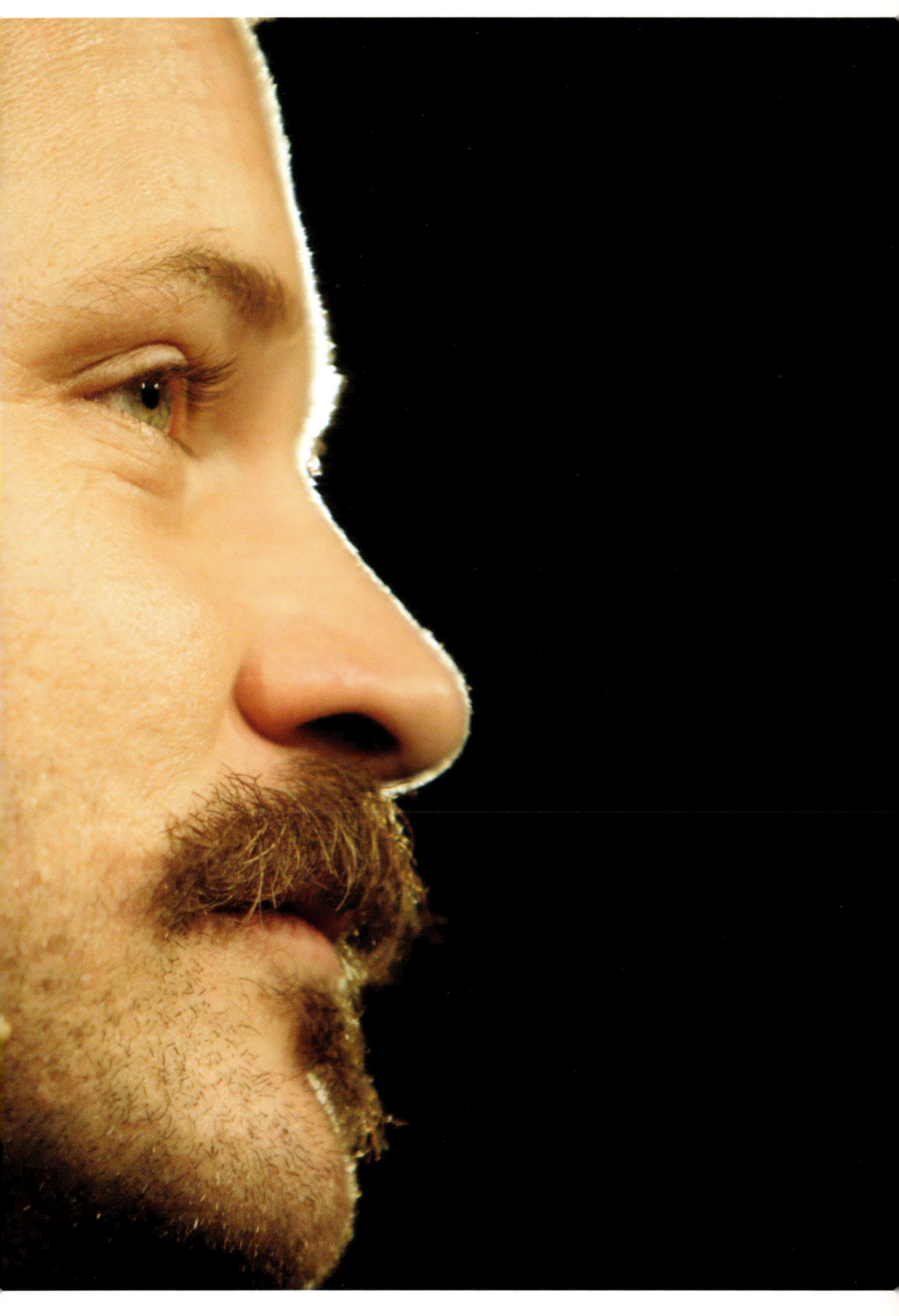

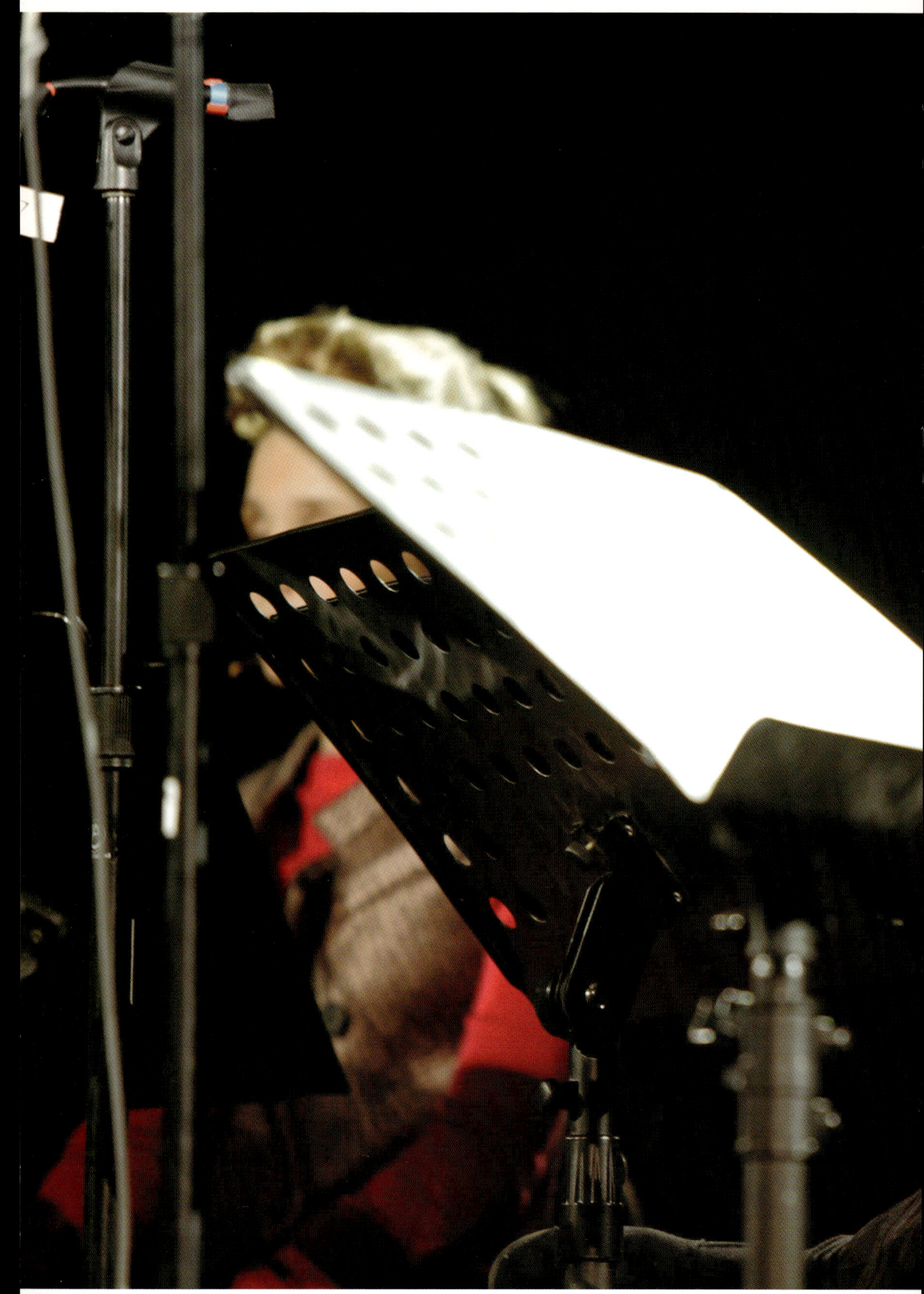

LAUDISI: HE IS TELLING THE TRUTH. BUT CLEARLY, AS FAR AS SHE IS CONCERNED SO IS SIGNORA FROLA.

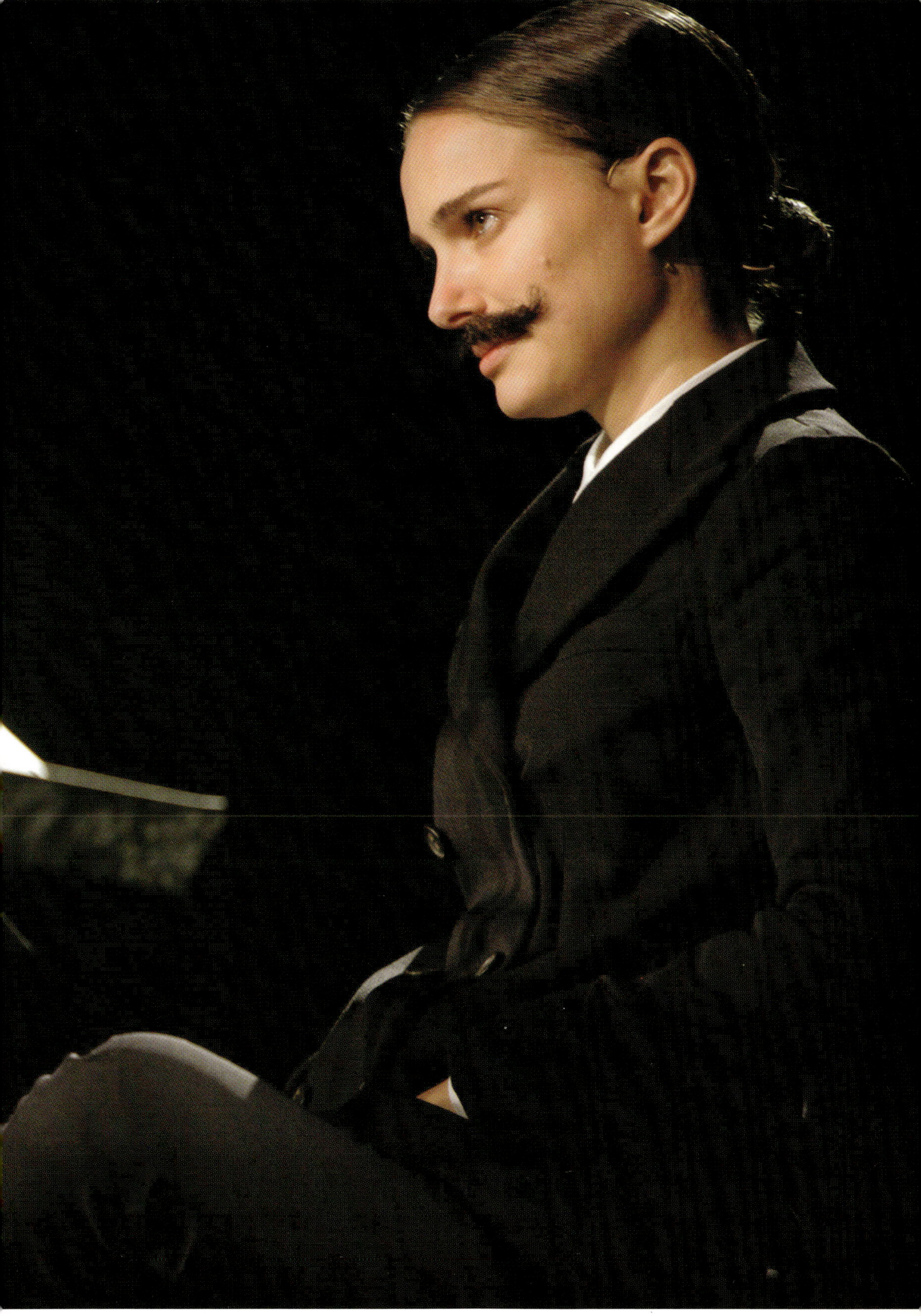

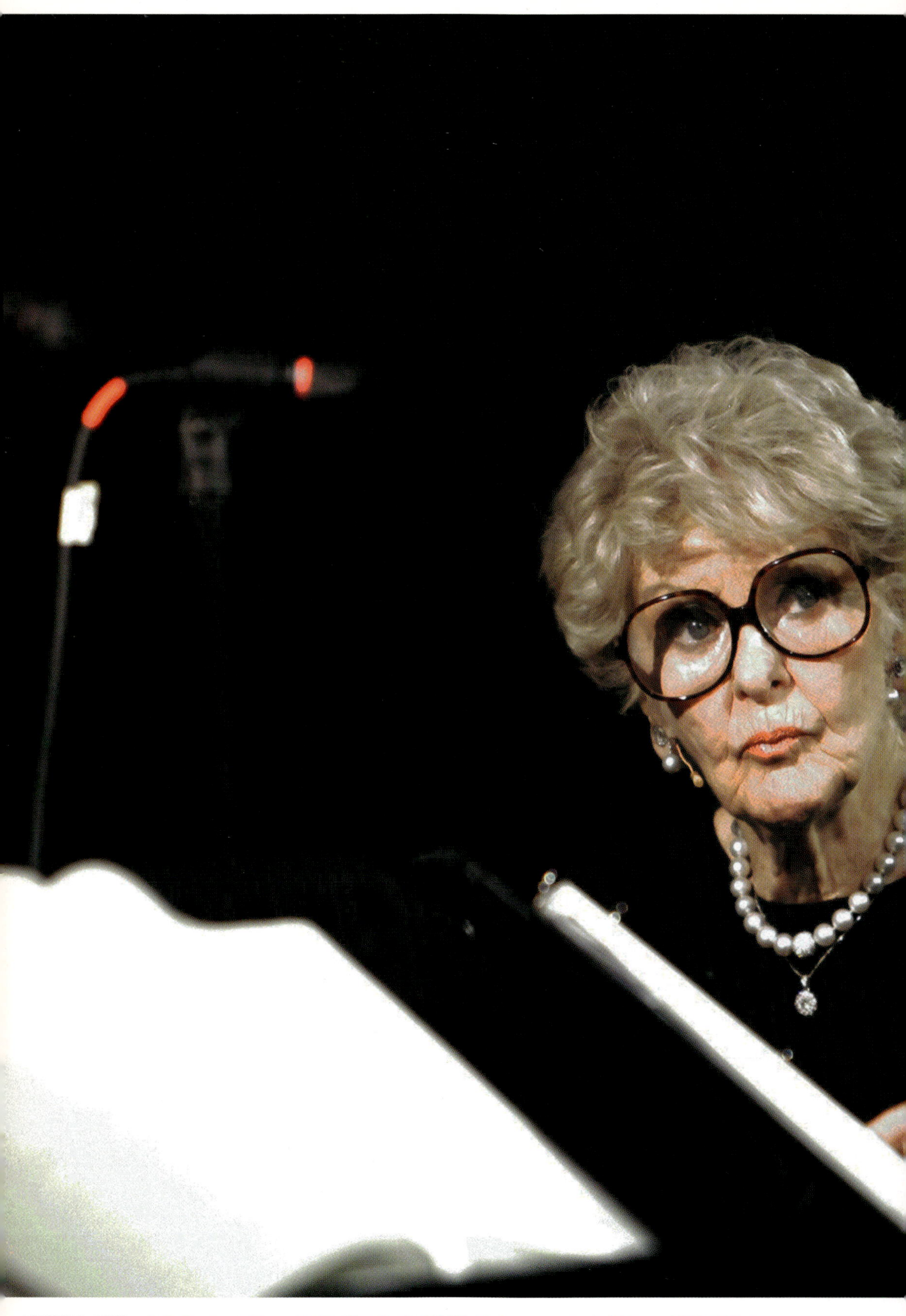

SIGNORA CINI: BUT THAT JUST...THAT MEANS WE DON'T KNOW ANYTHING STILL. DEFINITELY.

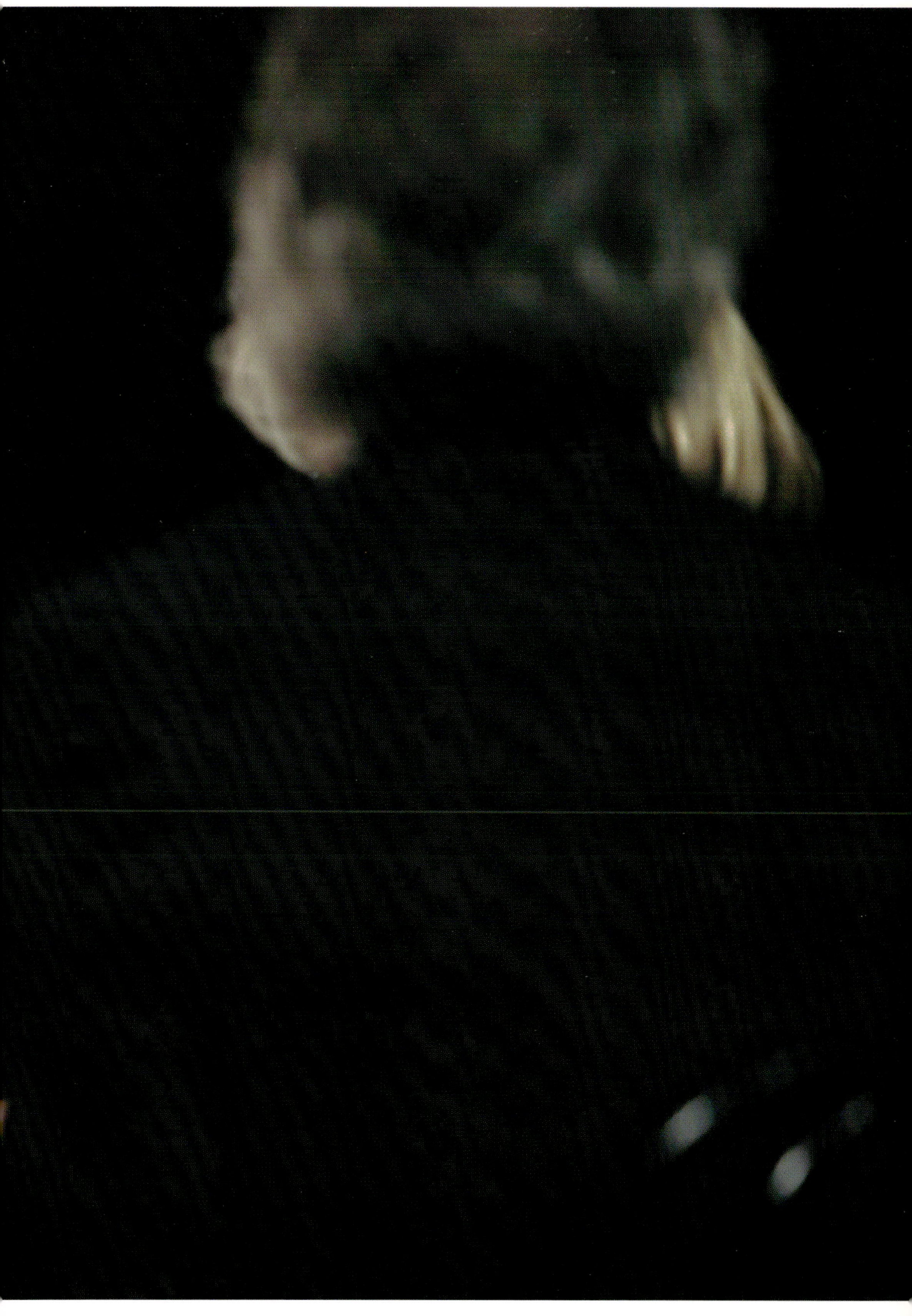

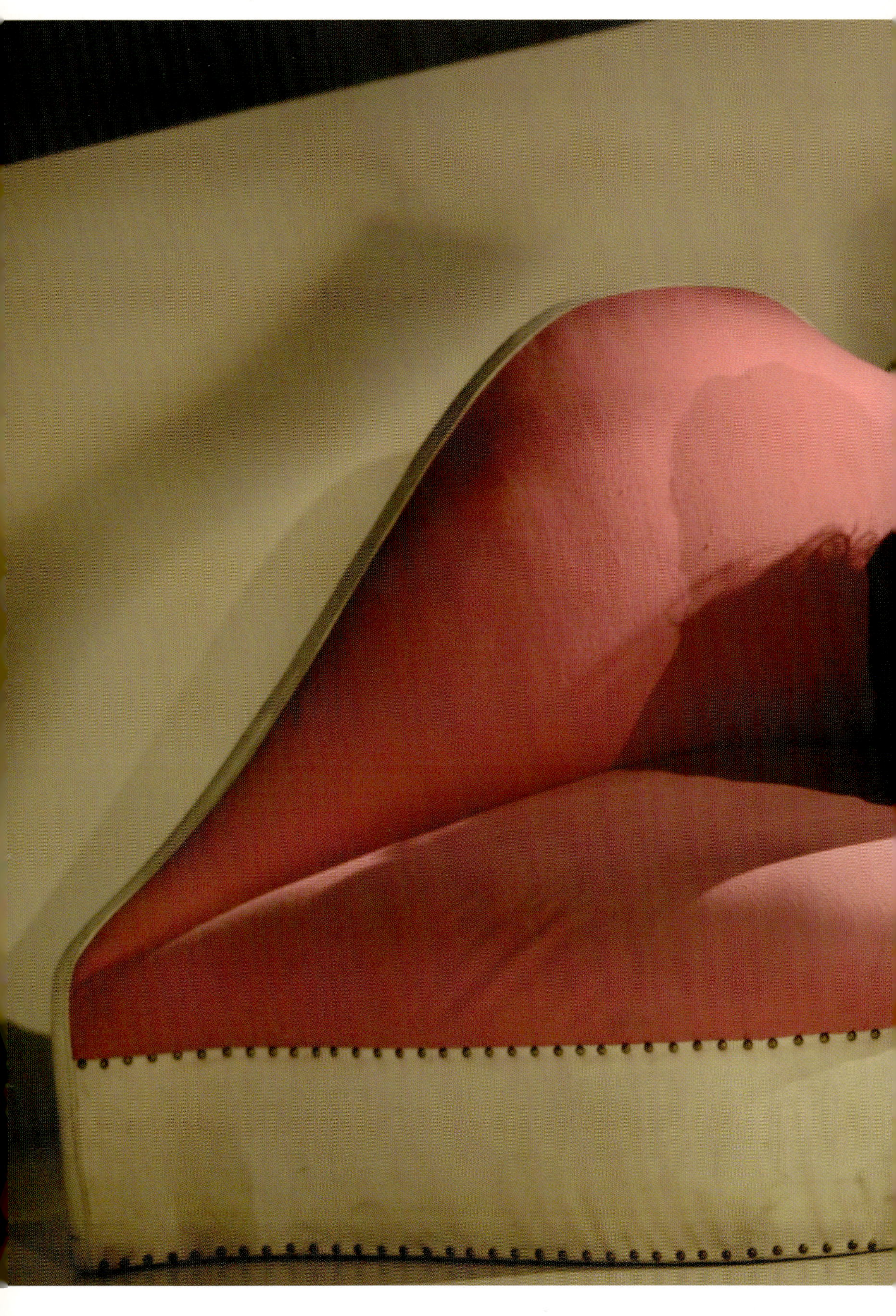

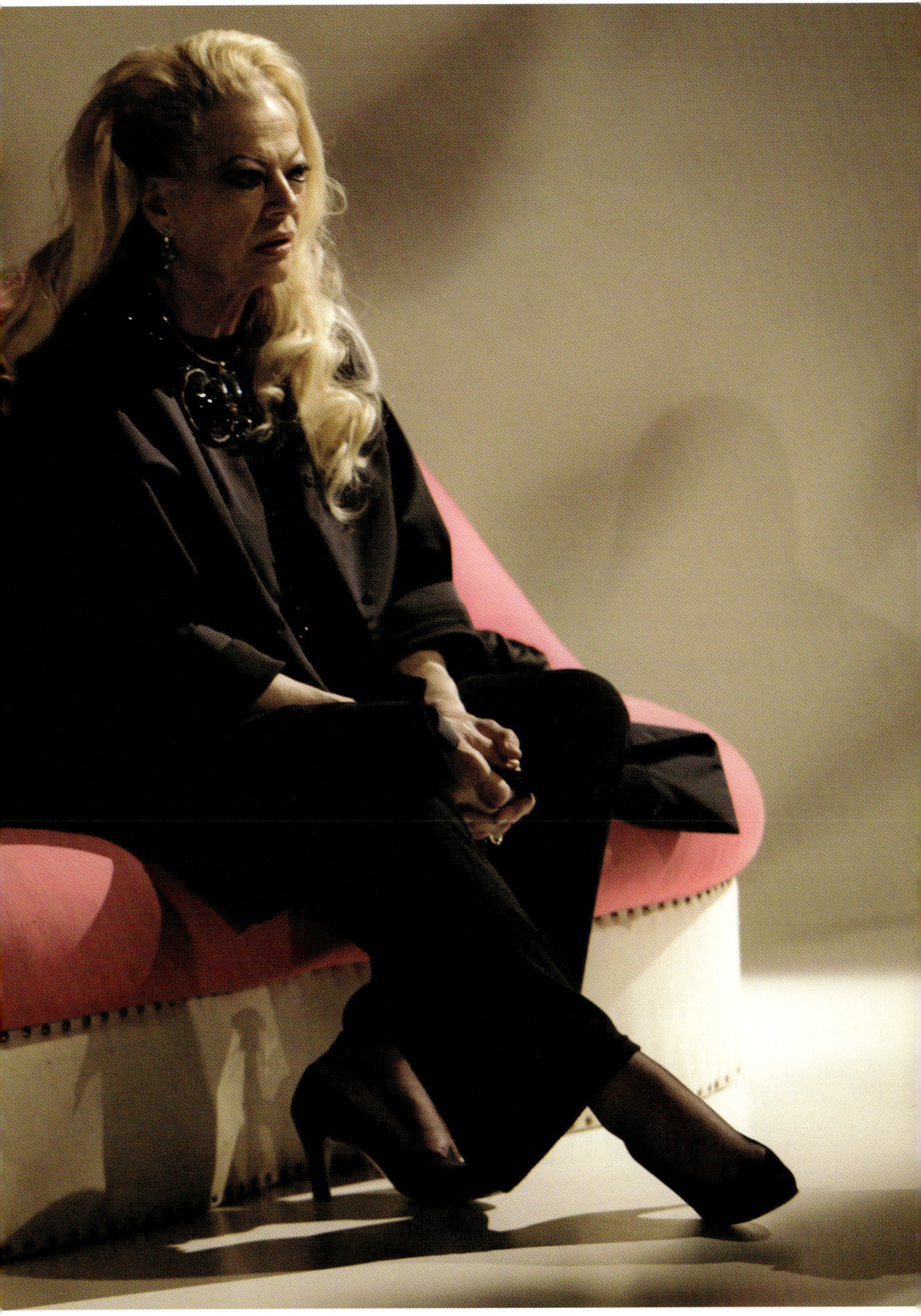

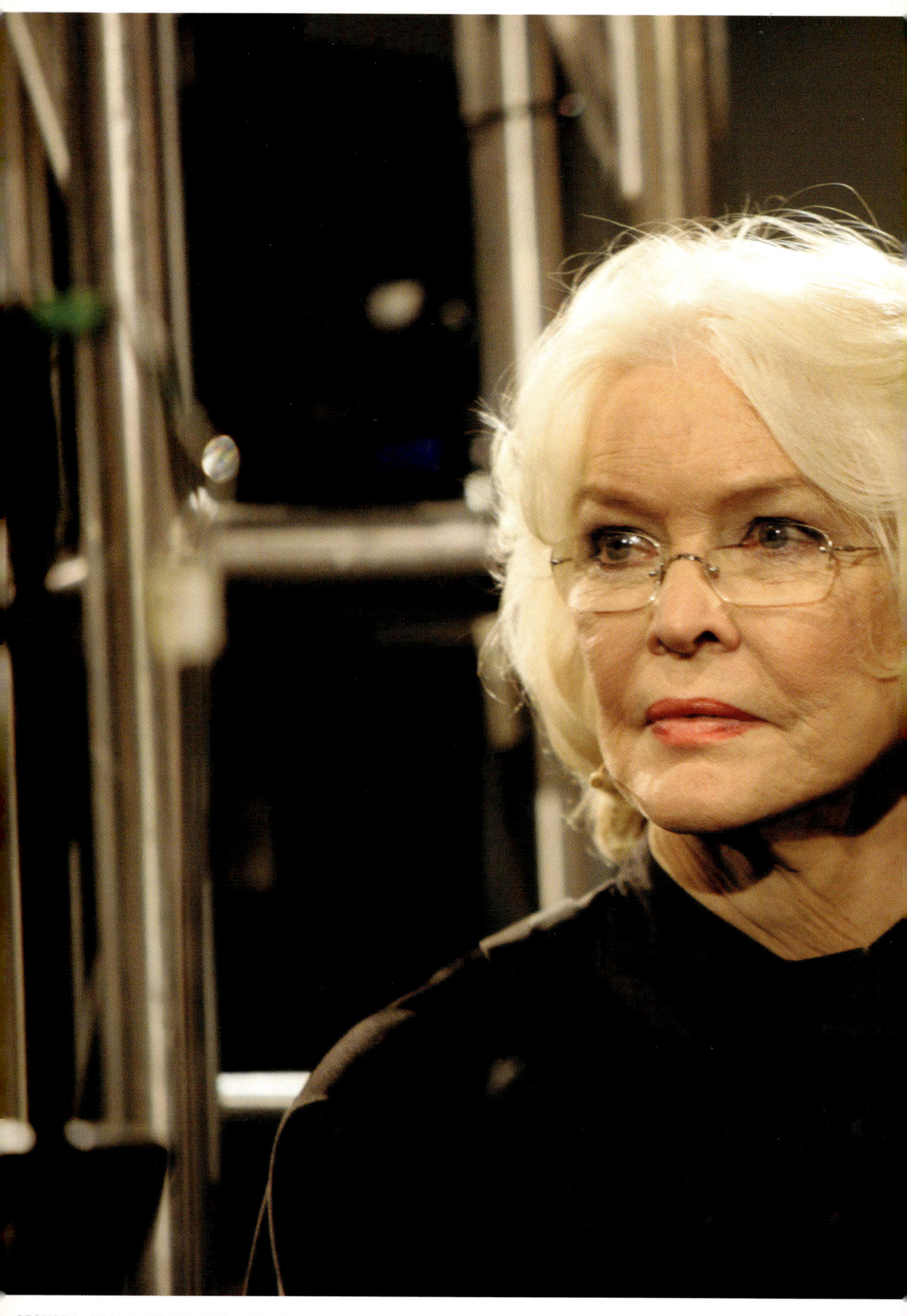
SIGNORA FROLA: THEN WHY ARE WE ALL FORCED TO EXPLAIN THE WAY WE LIVE? IF IT HAS NO BEARING ON HIS

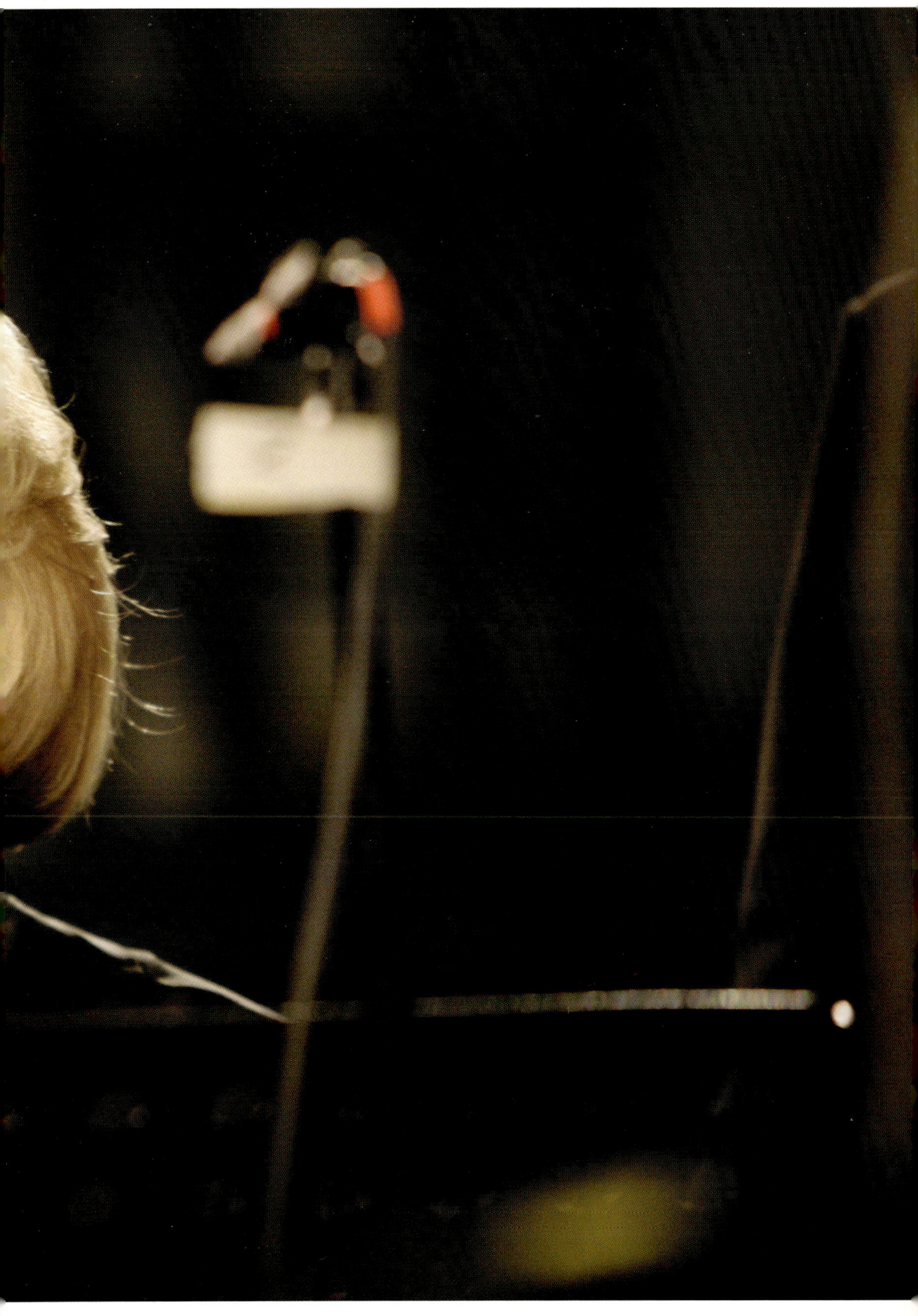

ROSPECTS? AND WE TELL THESE STORIES TO AVOID THE TRUTH.

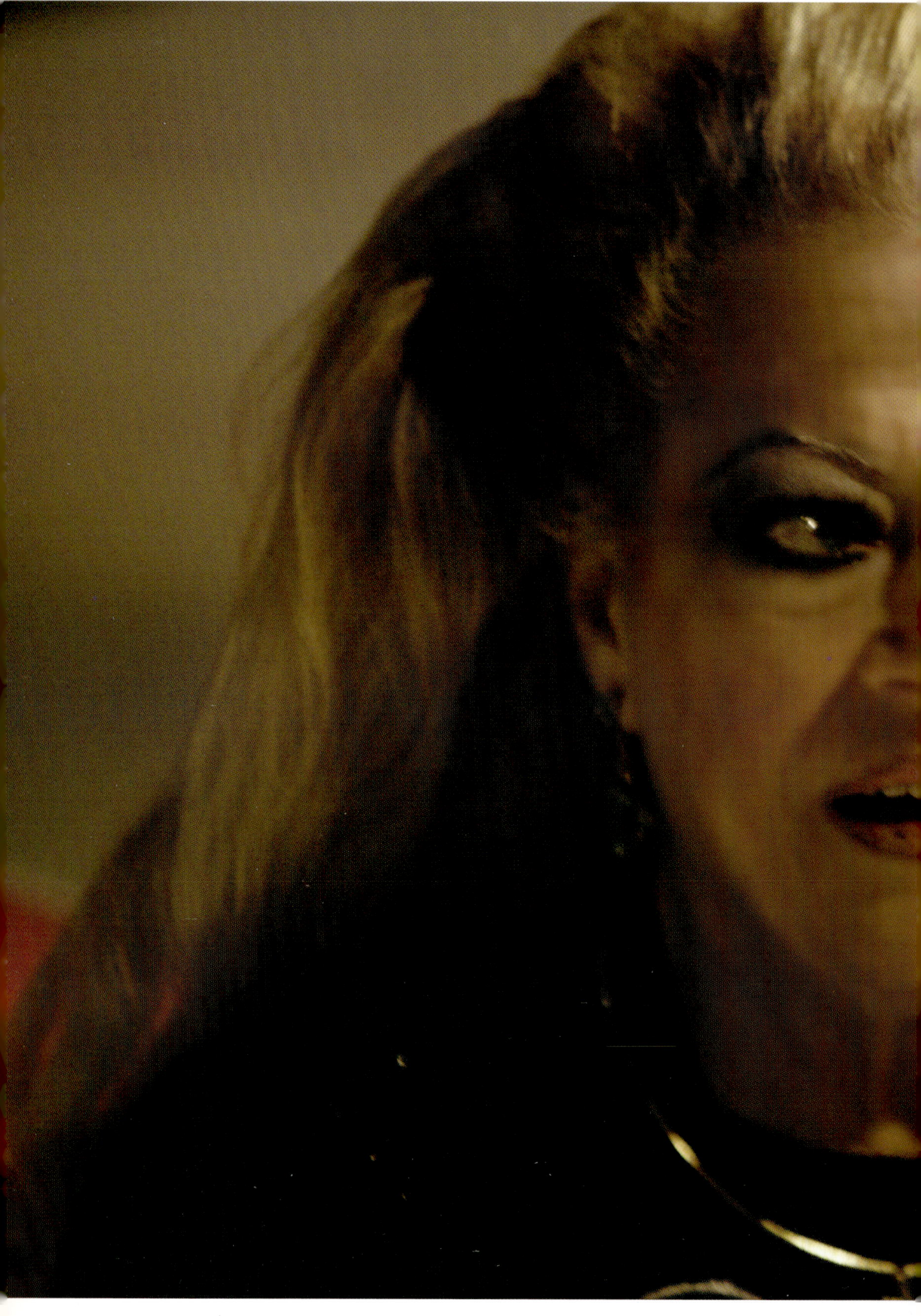

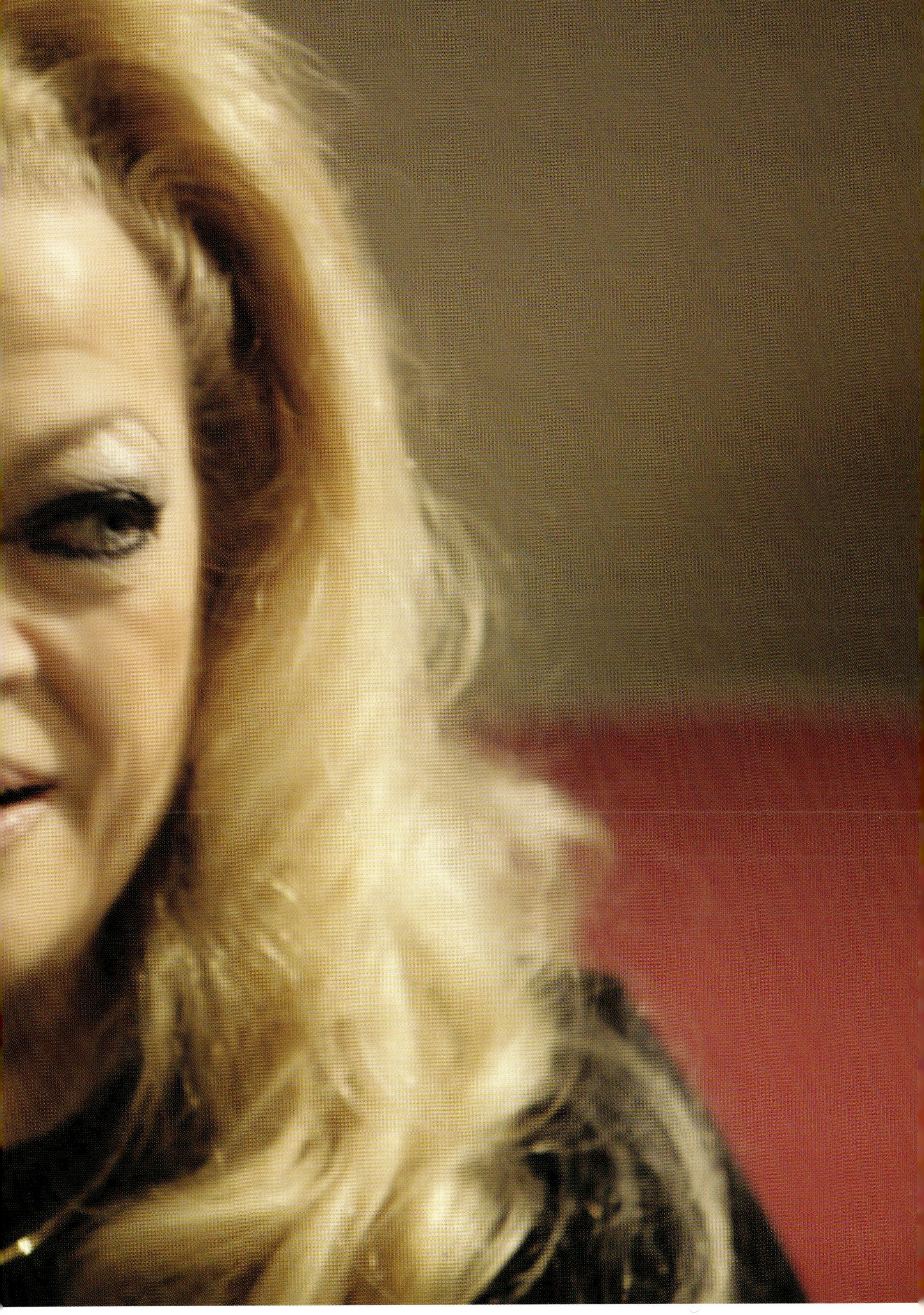

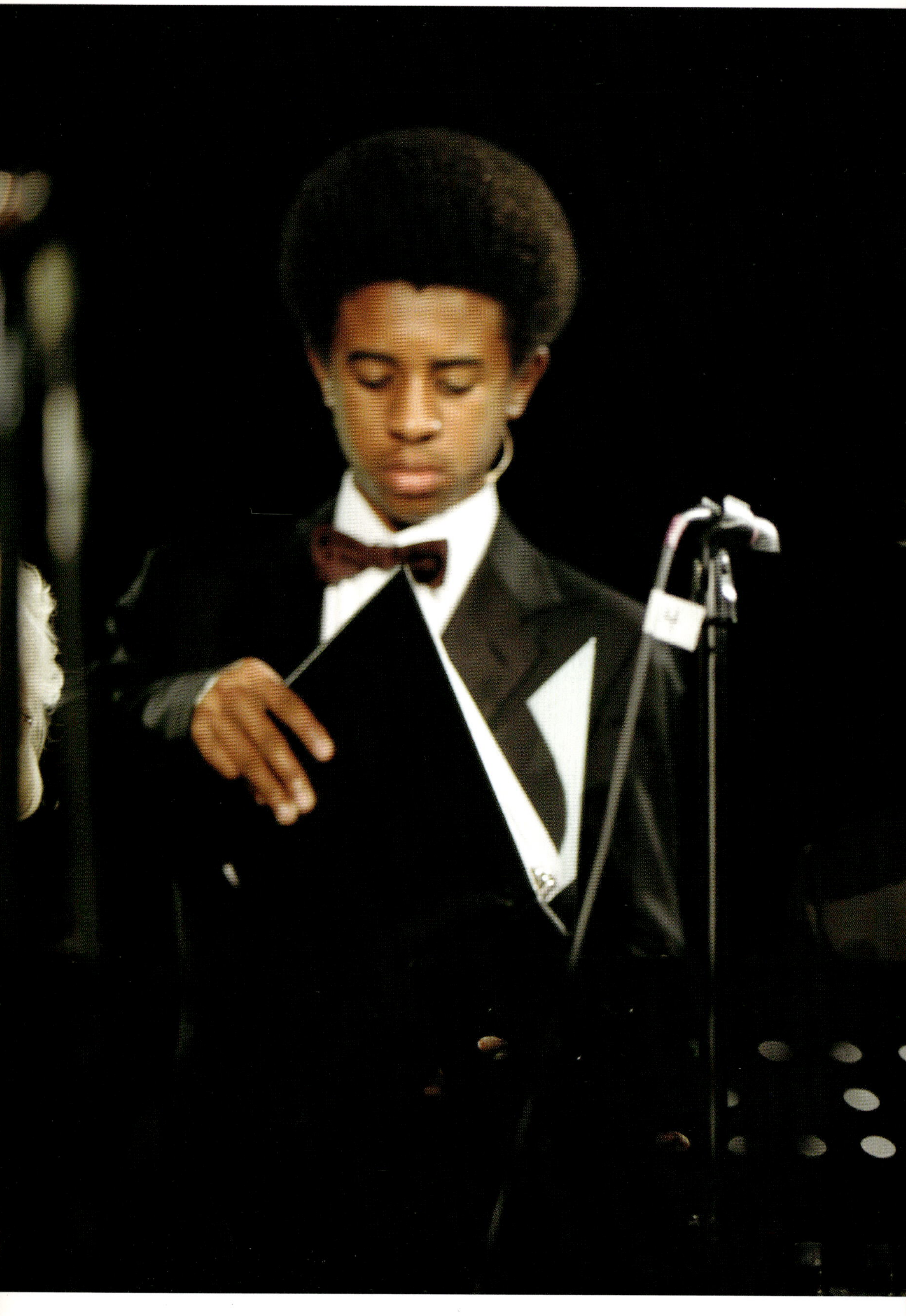

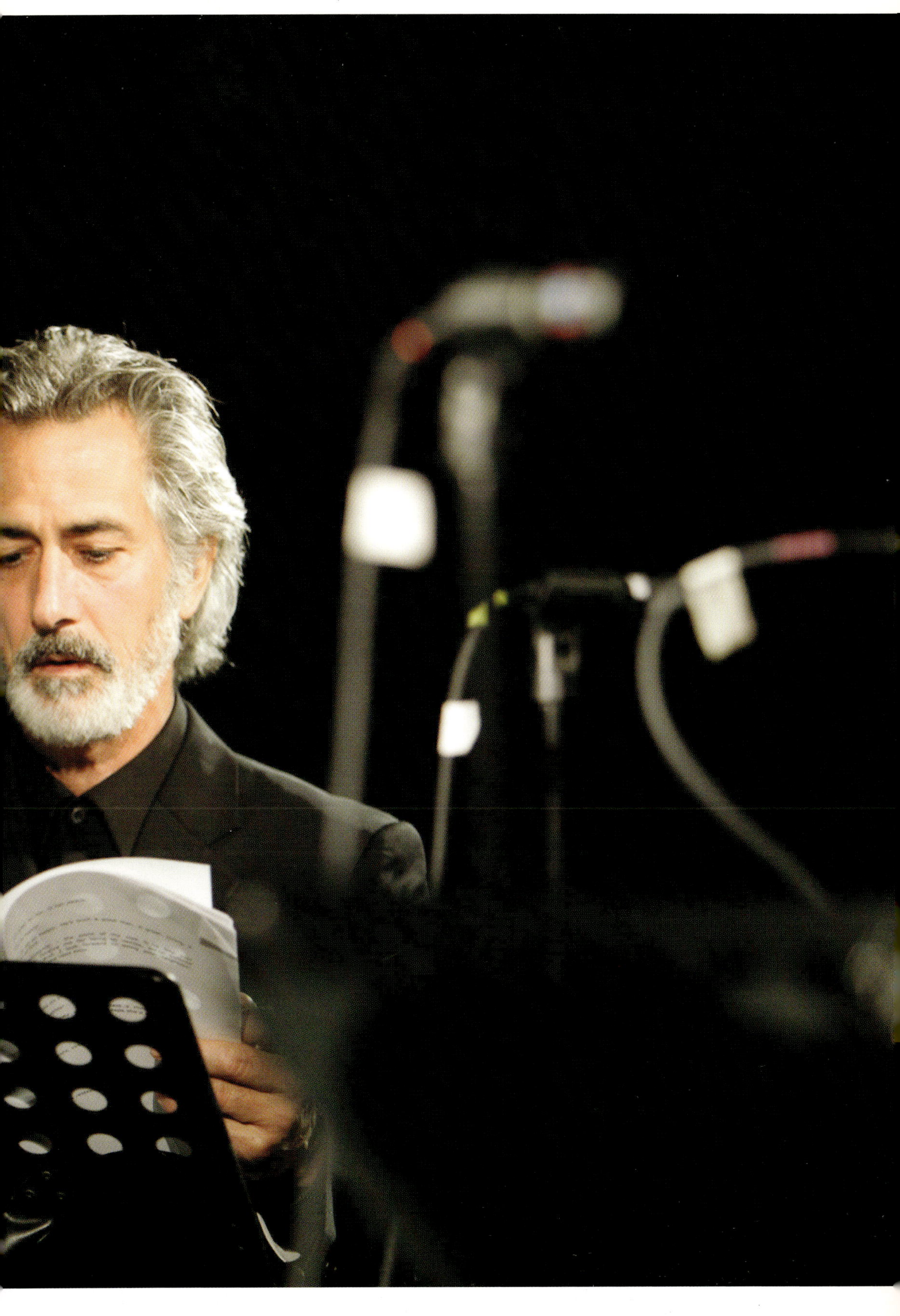

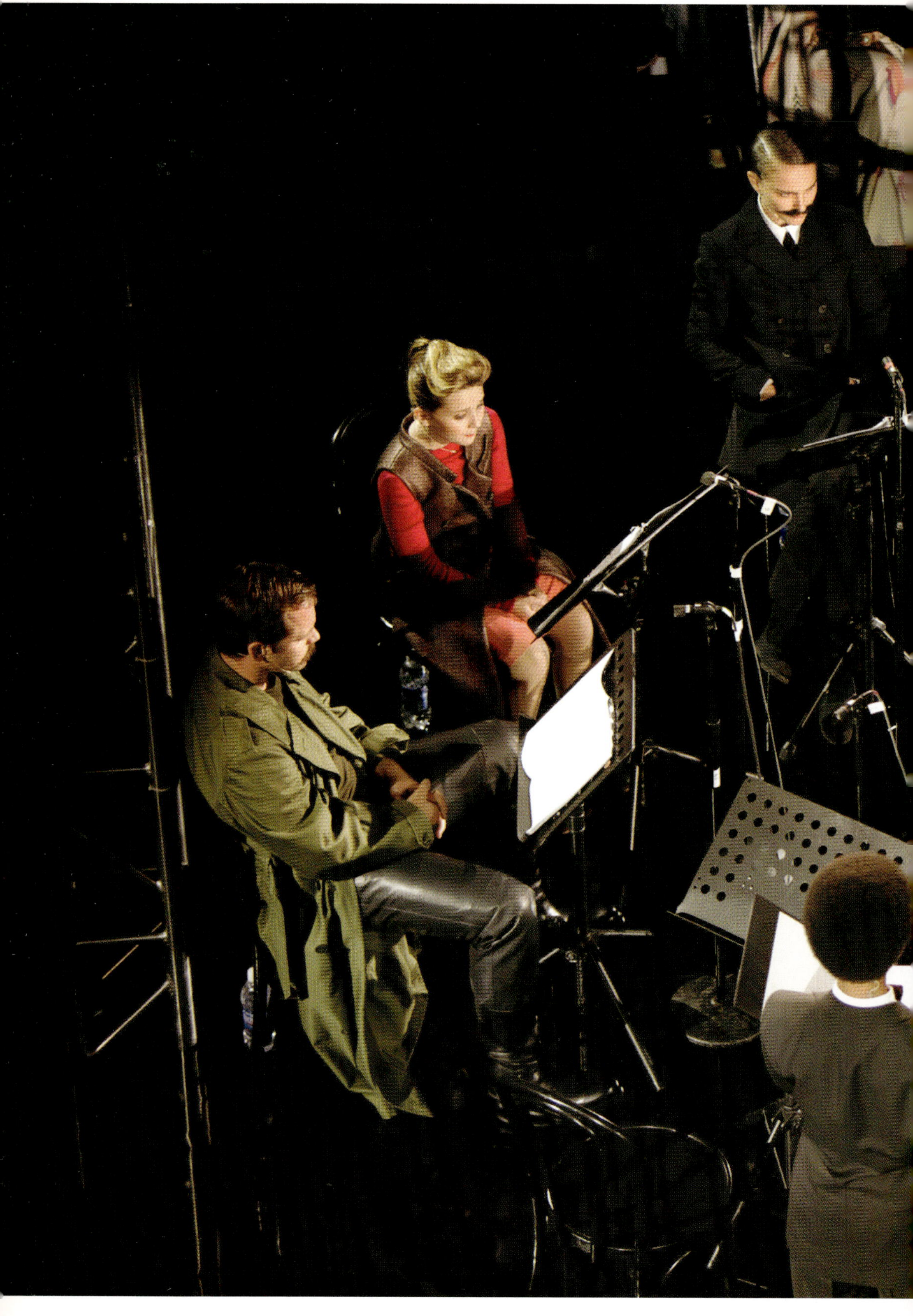

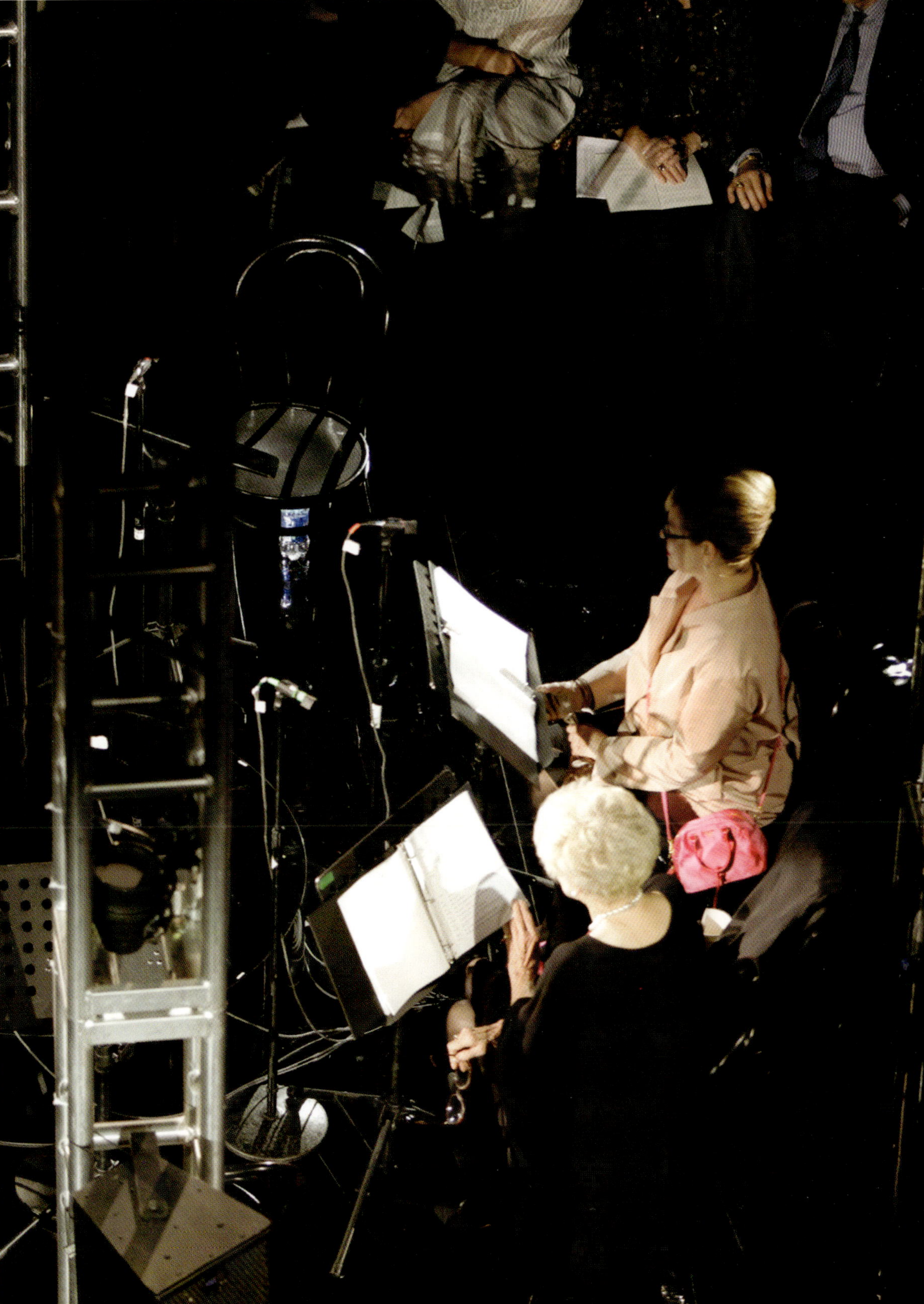

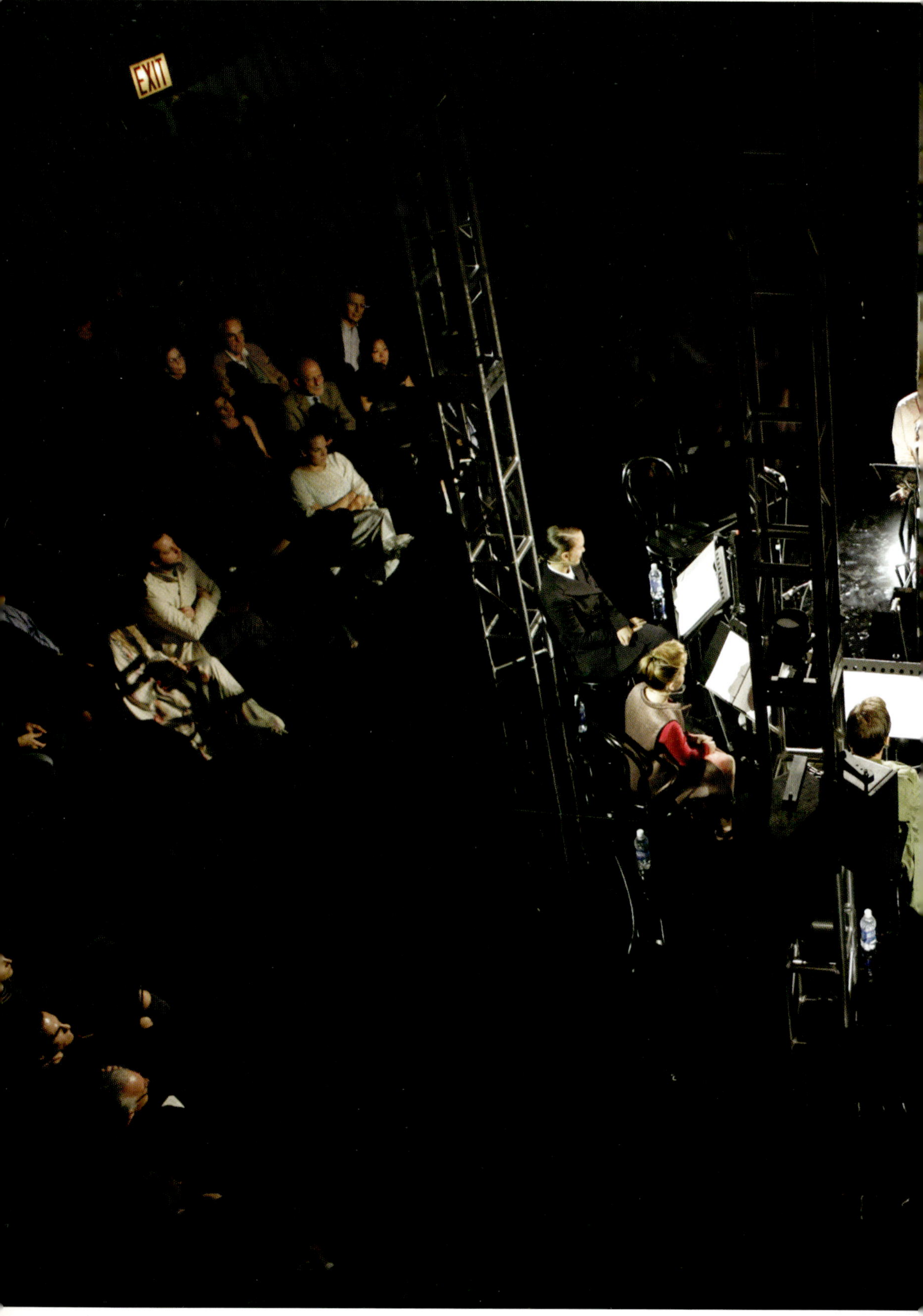

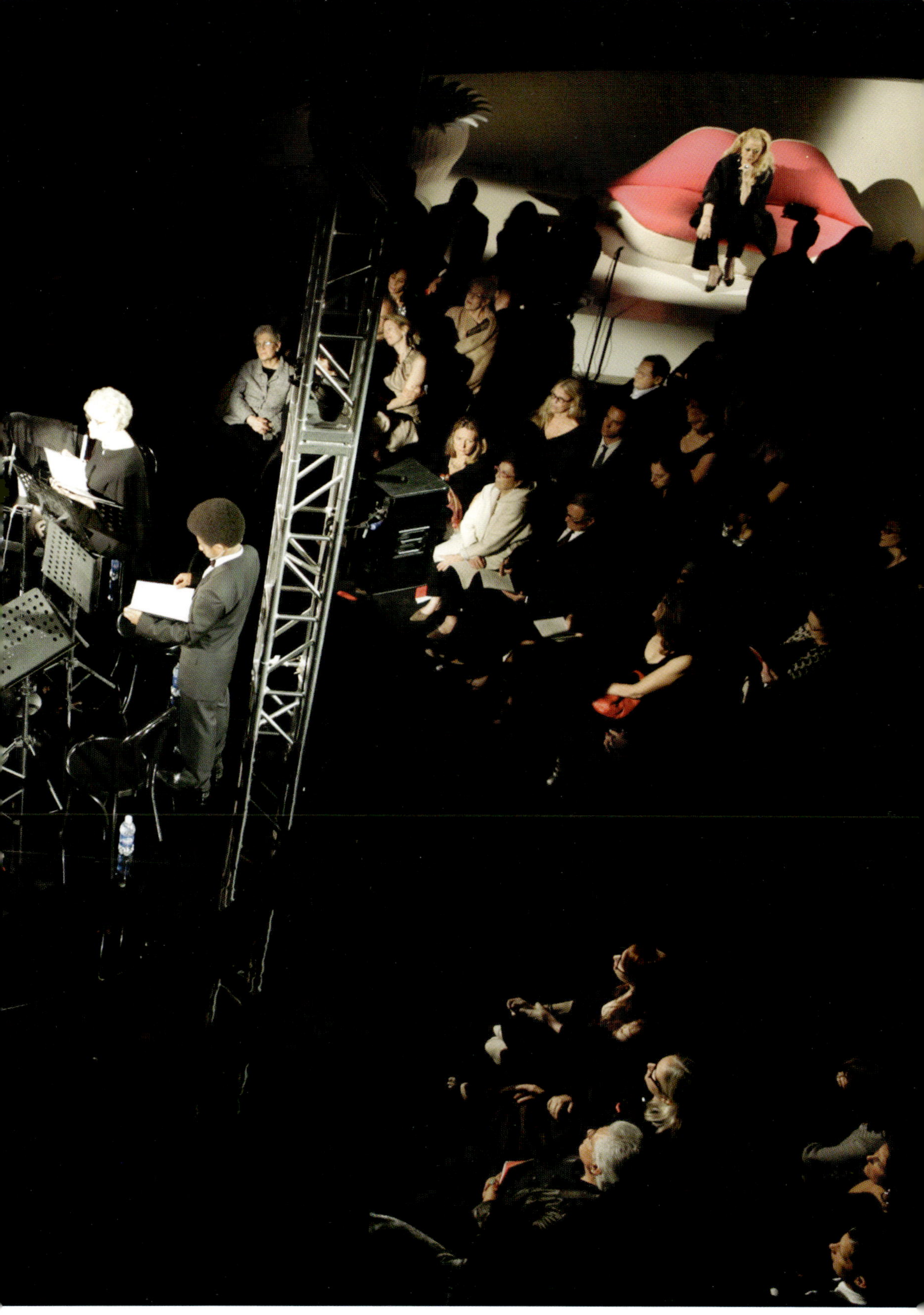

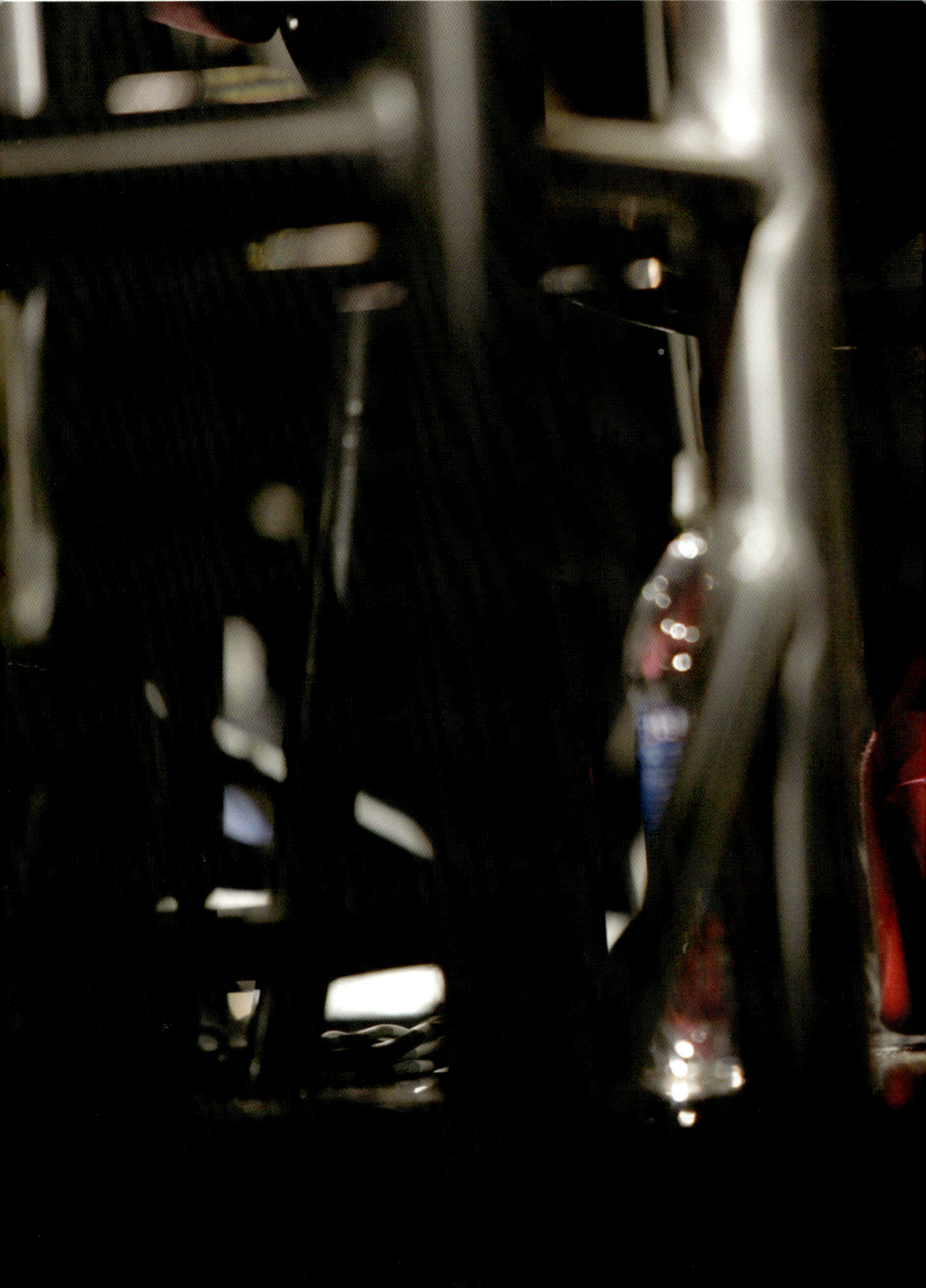

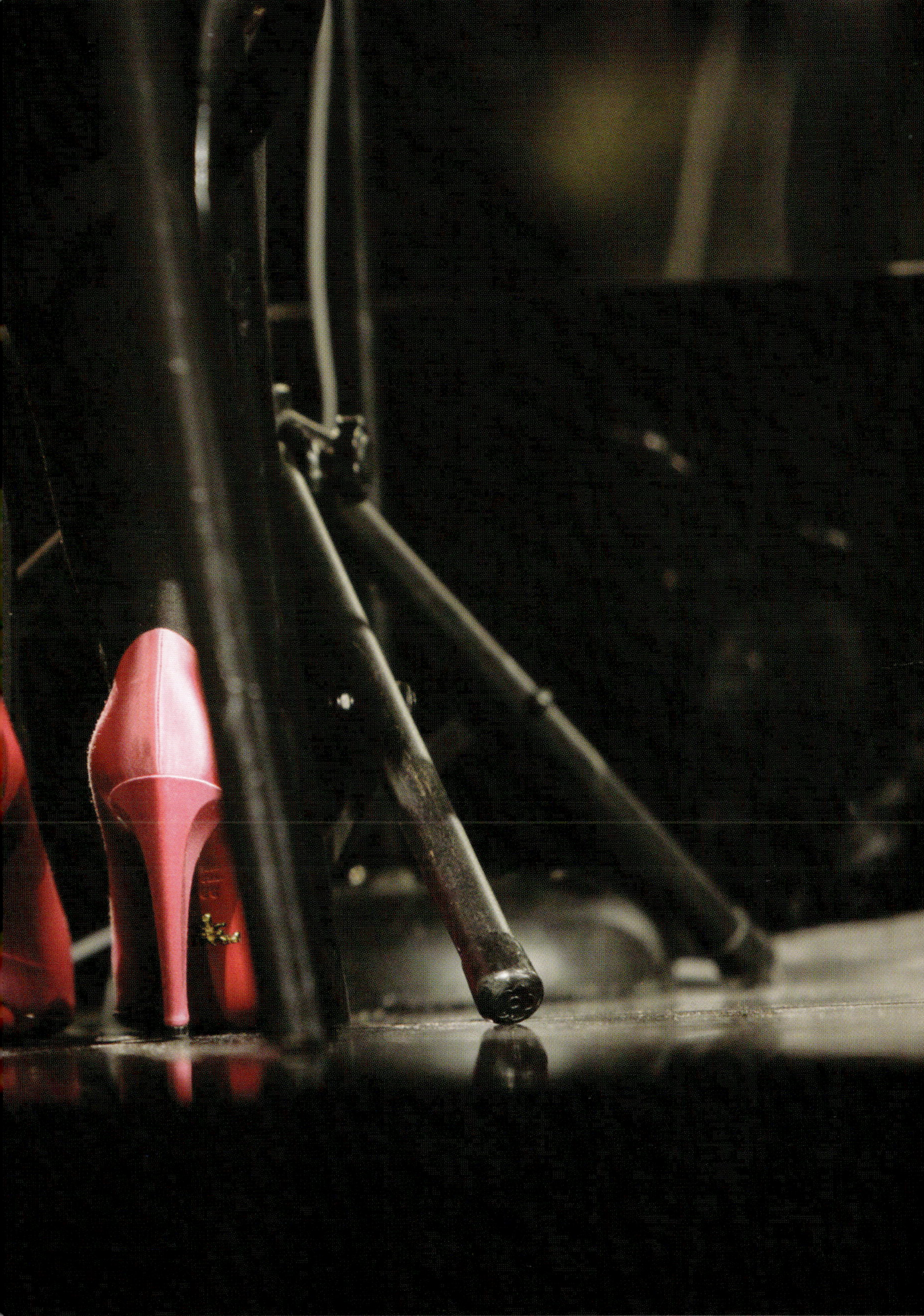

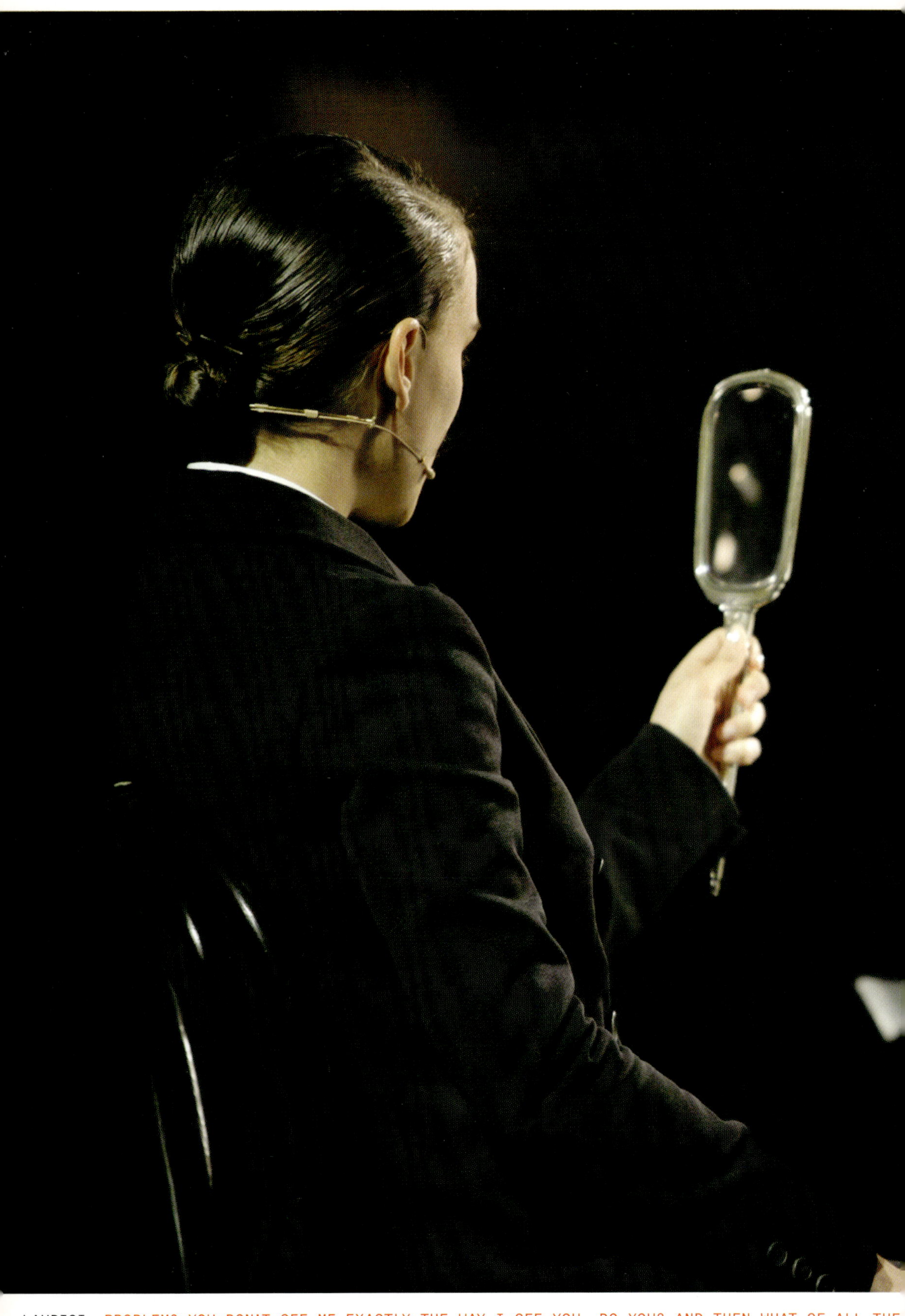

LAUDISI: PROBLEM? YOU DON'T SEE ME EXACTLY THE WAY I SEE YOU, DO YOU? AND THEN WHAT OF ALL THE

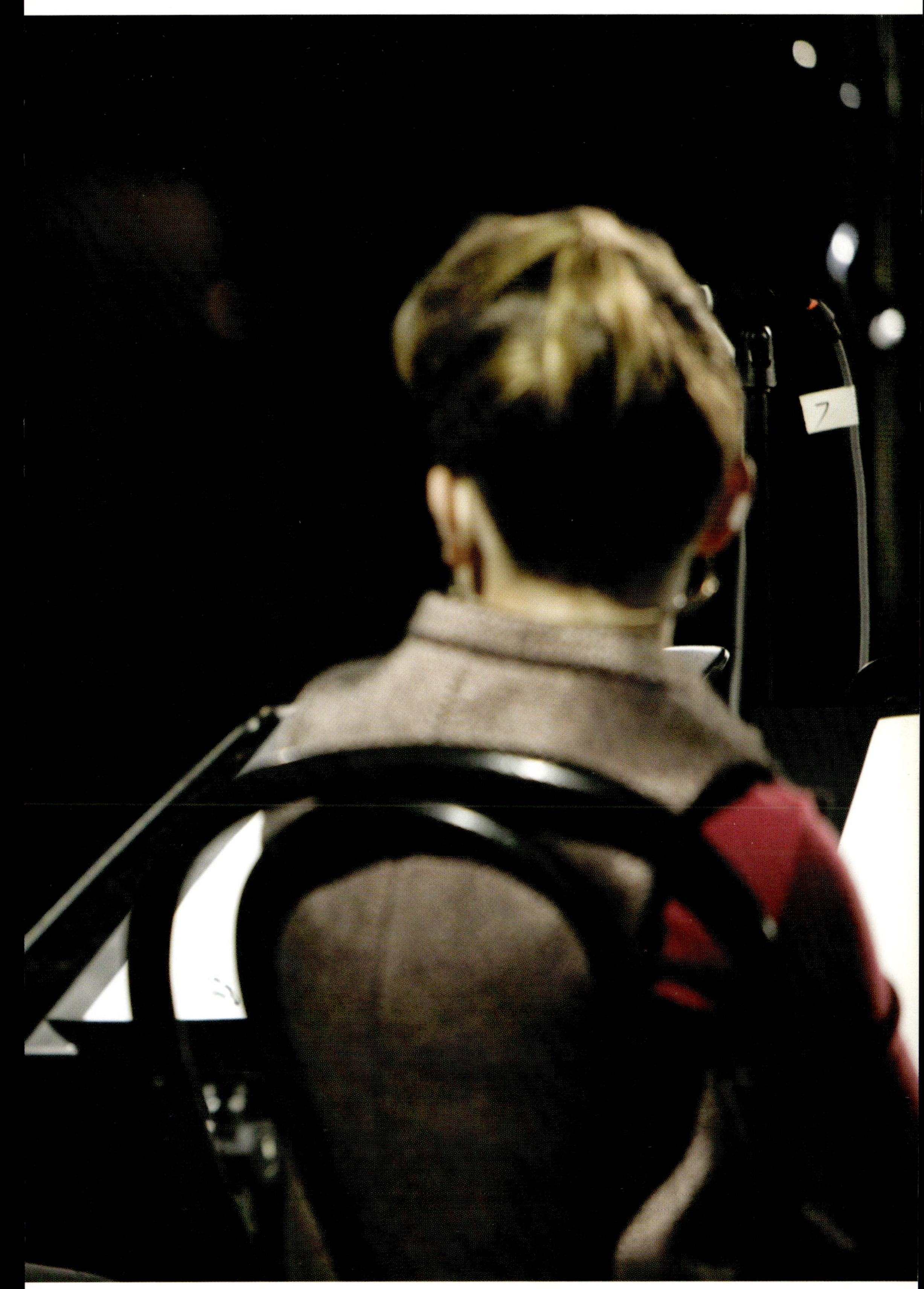
OTHERS? OTHERS? AND SO WHAT DO WE KNOW? WHAT DOES THAT MAKE US? SHADOWS? GHOSTS?

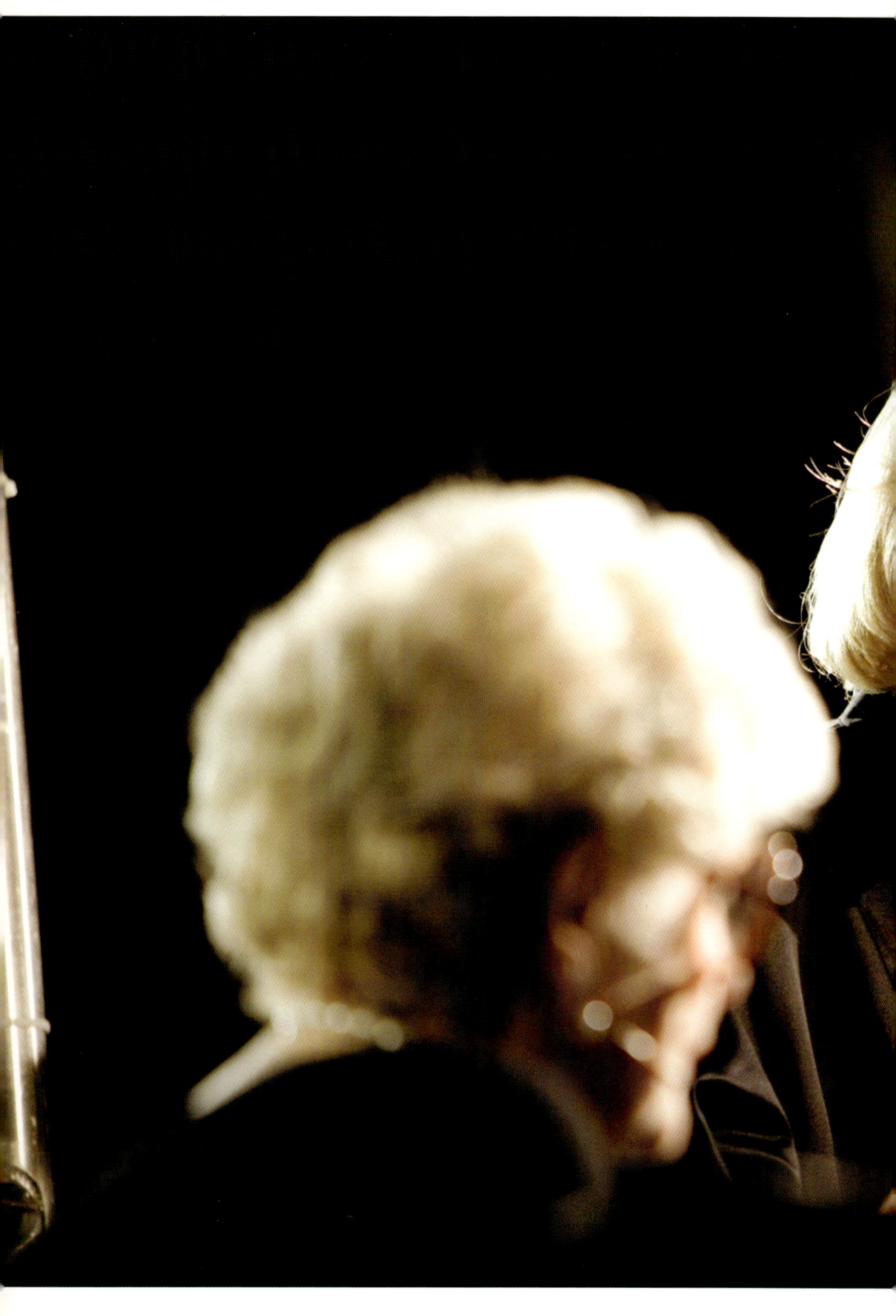

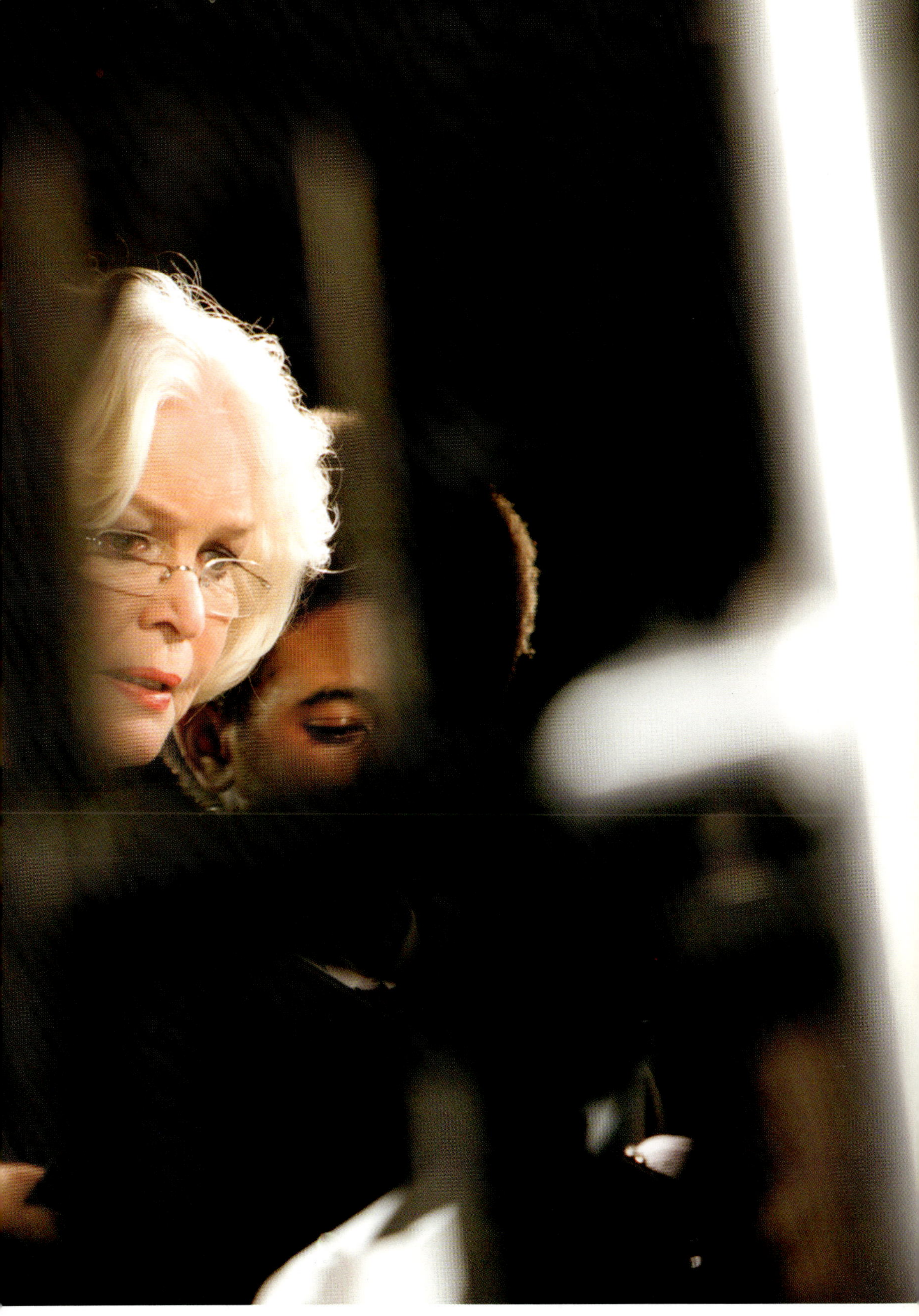

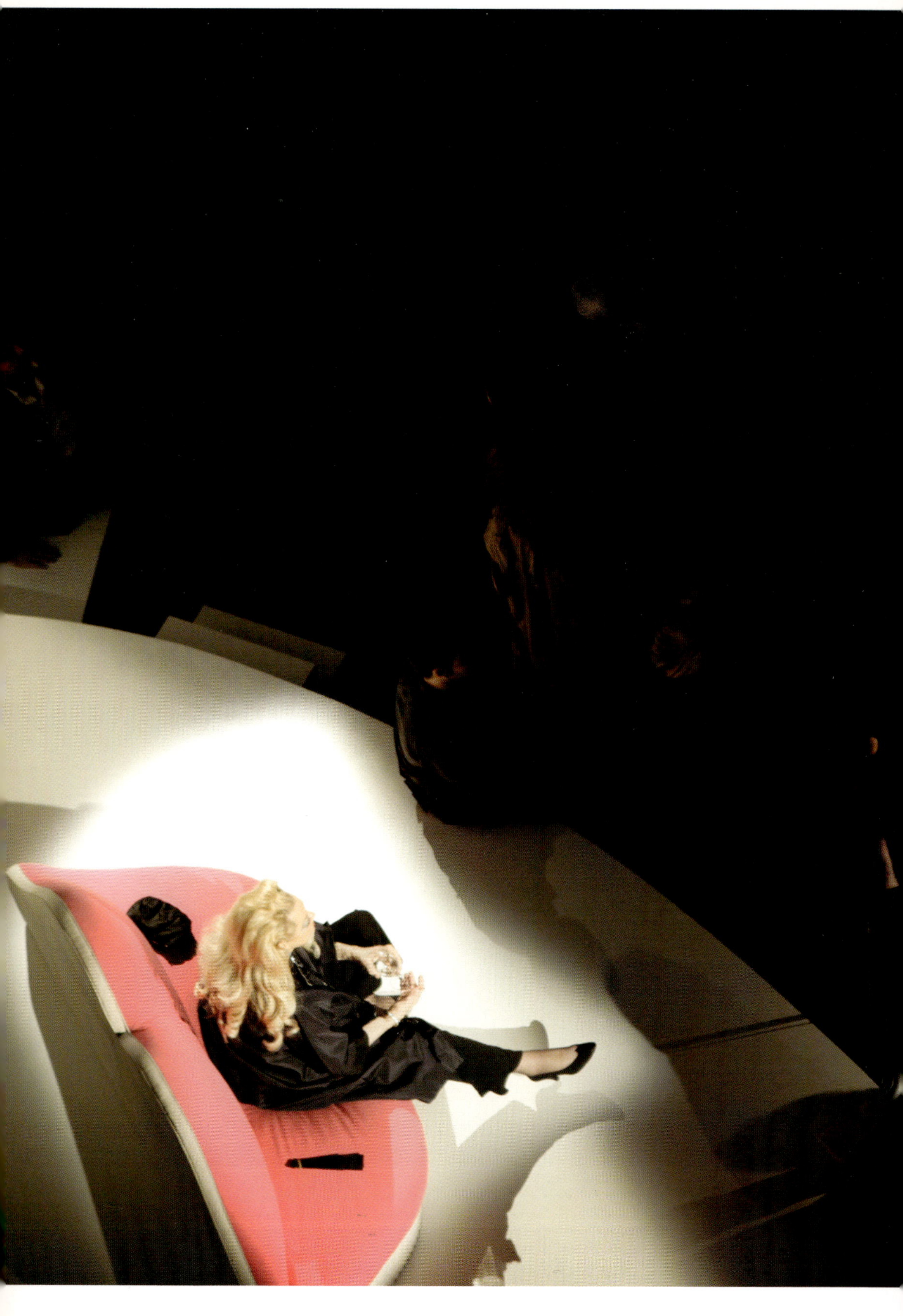

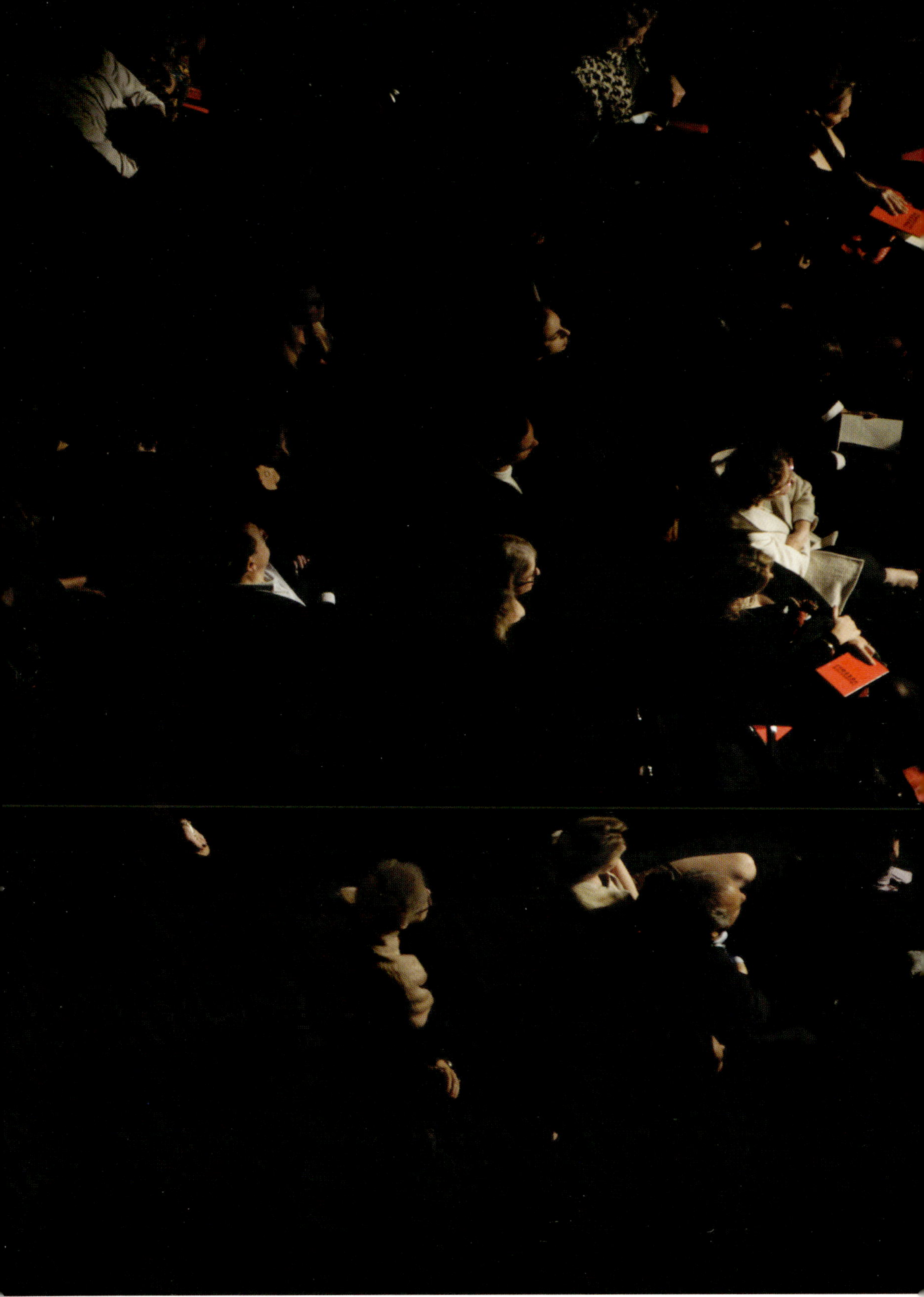

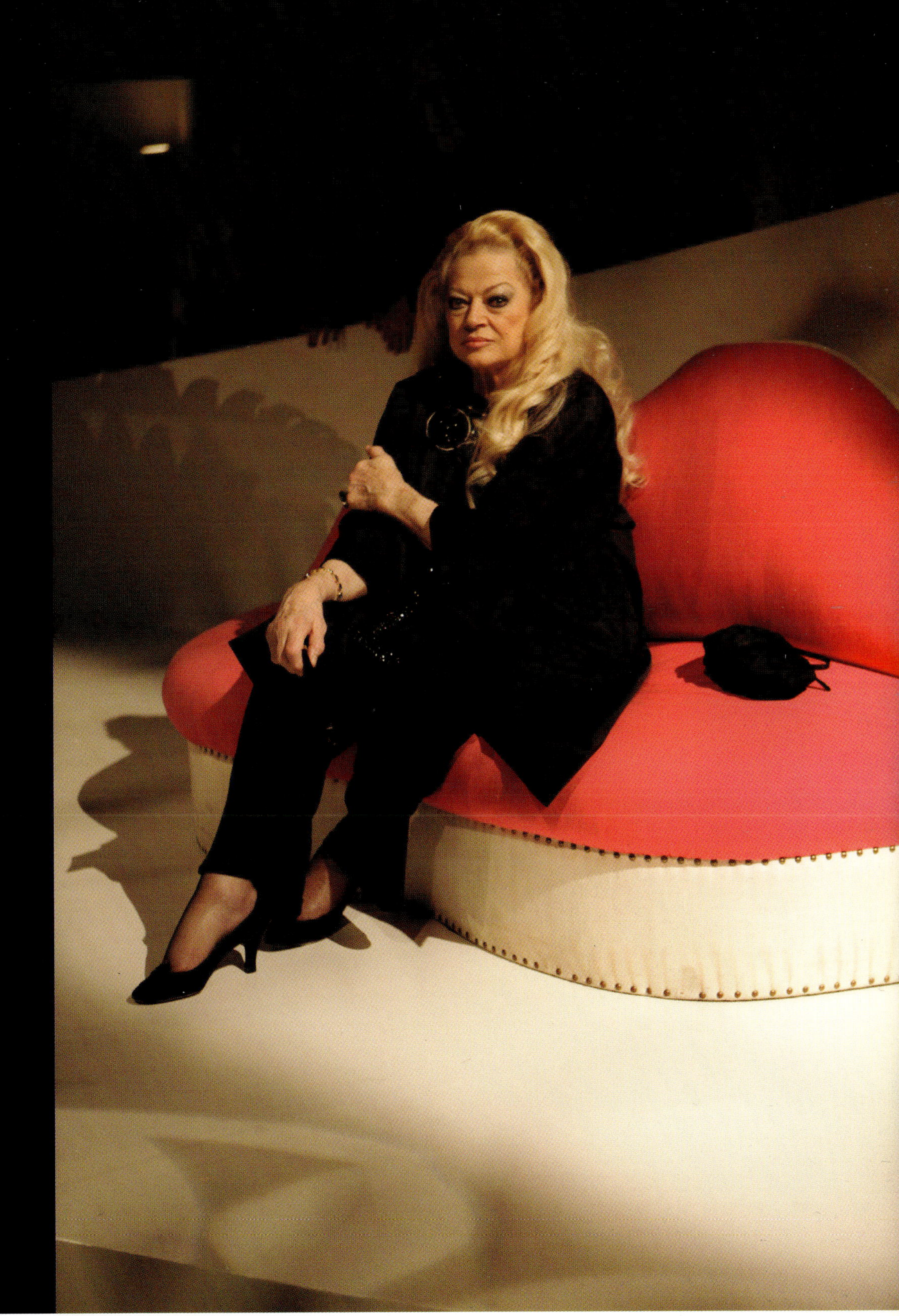

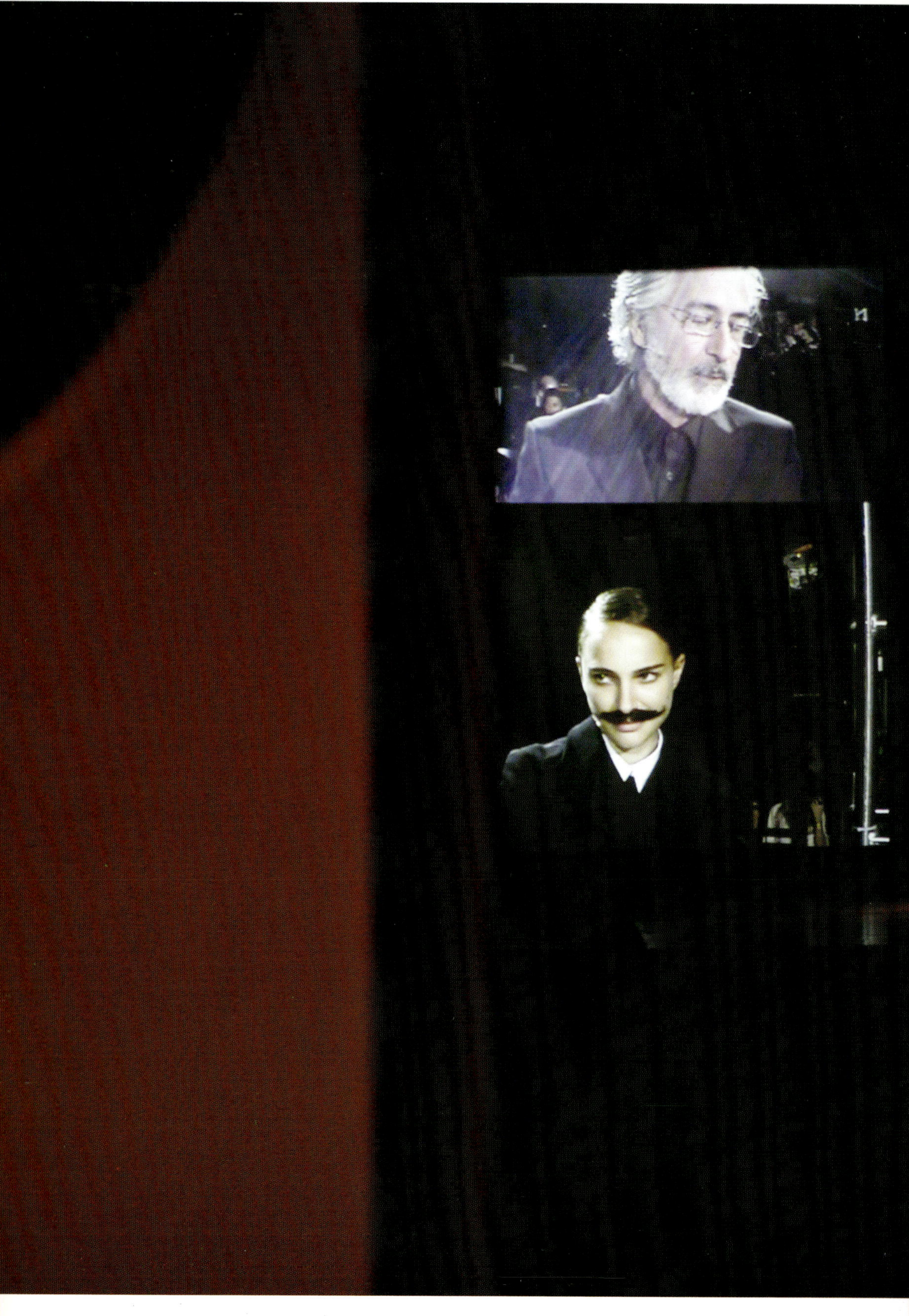

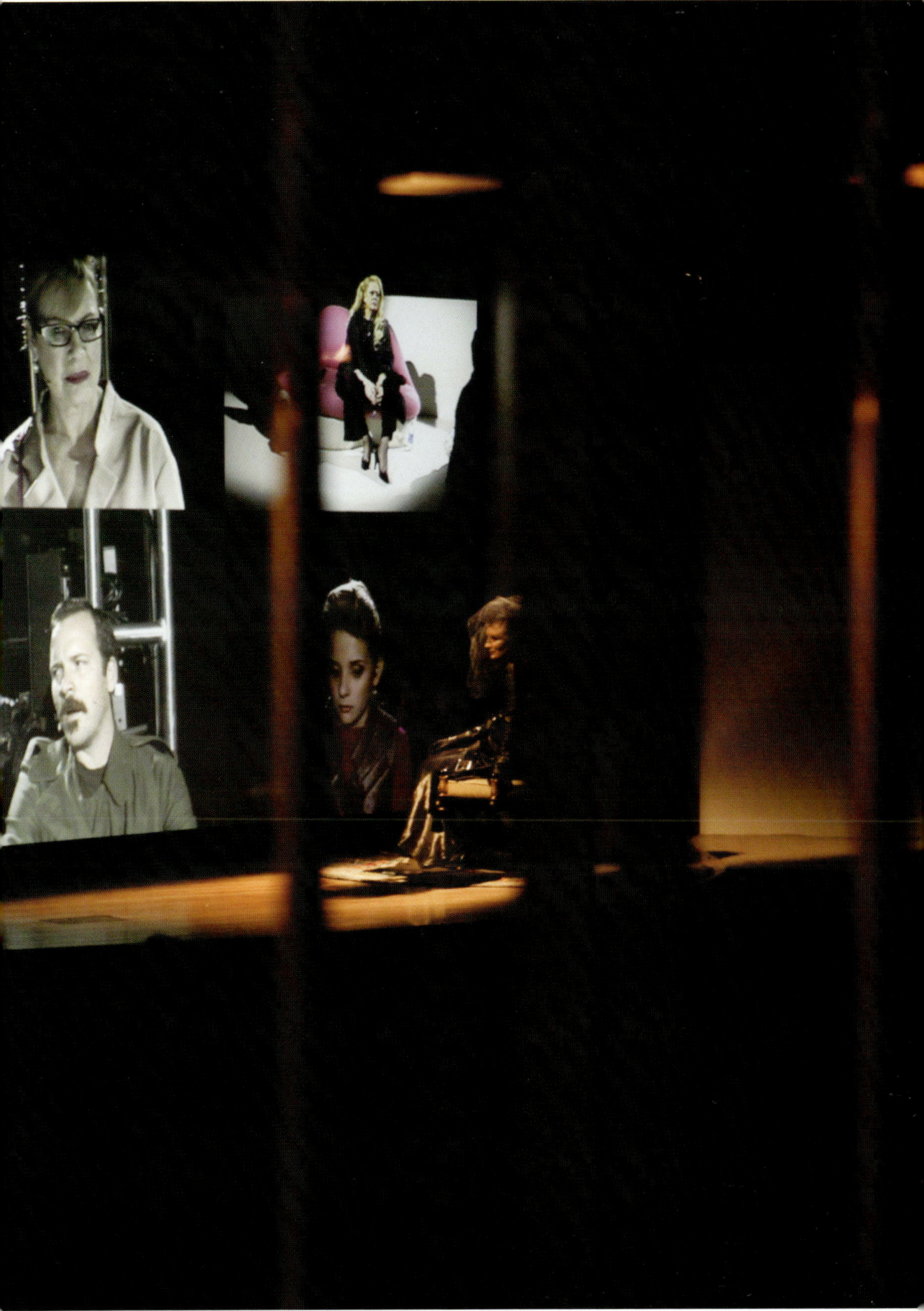

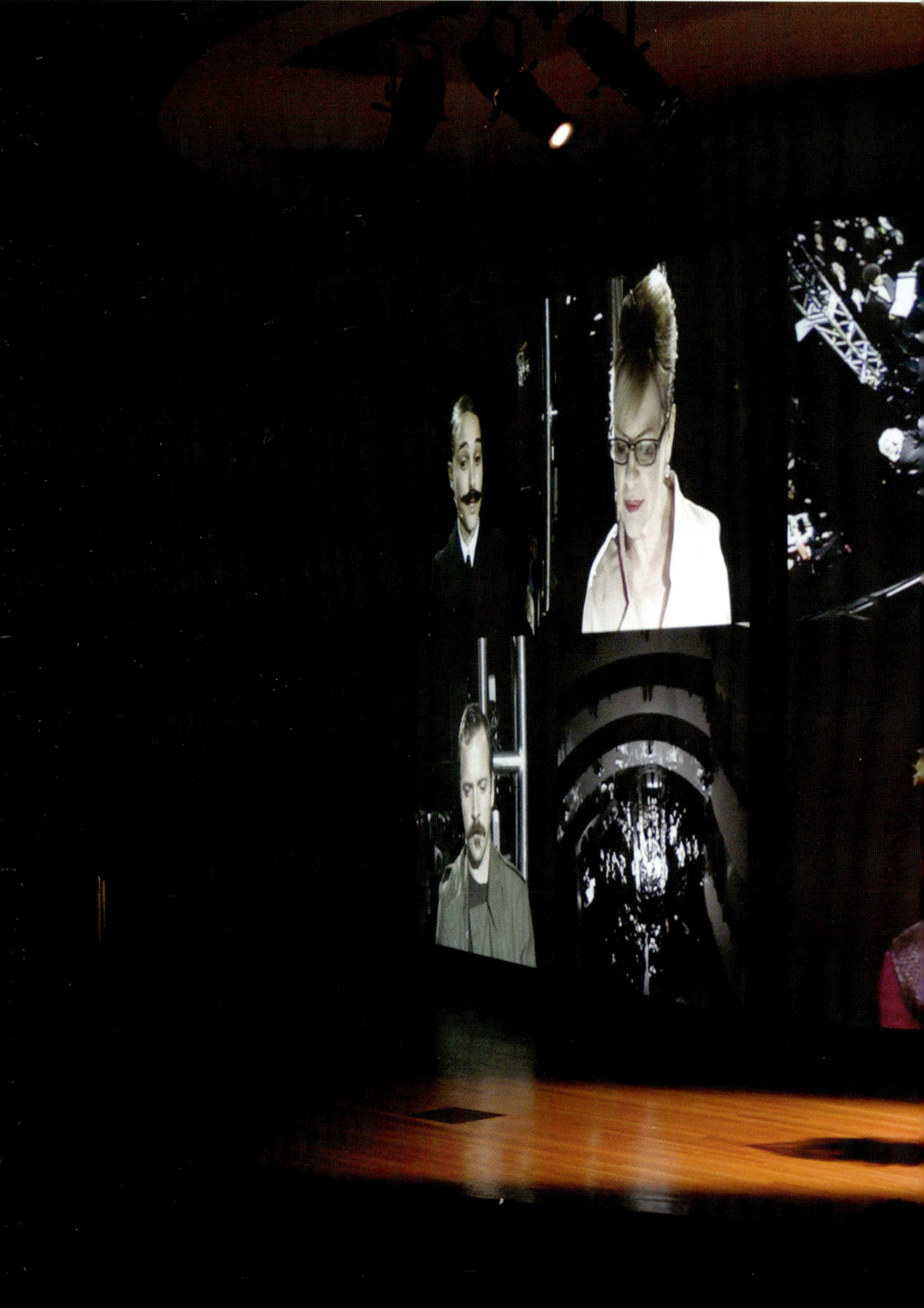

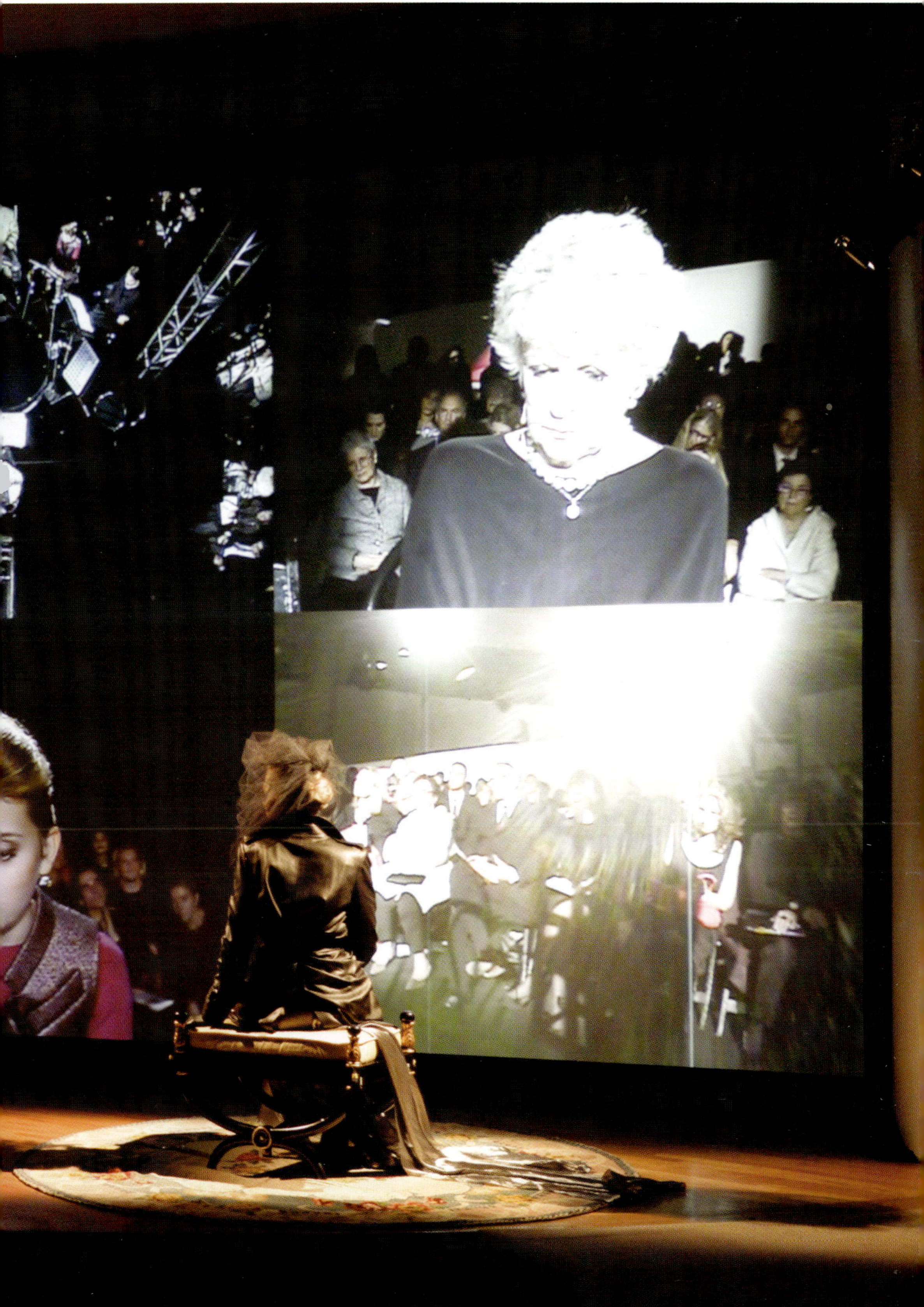

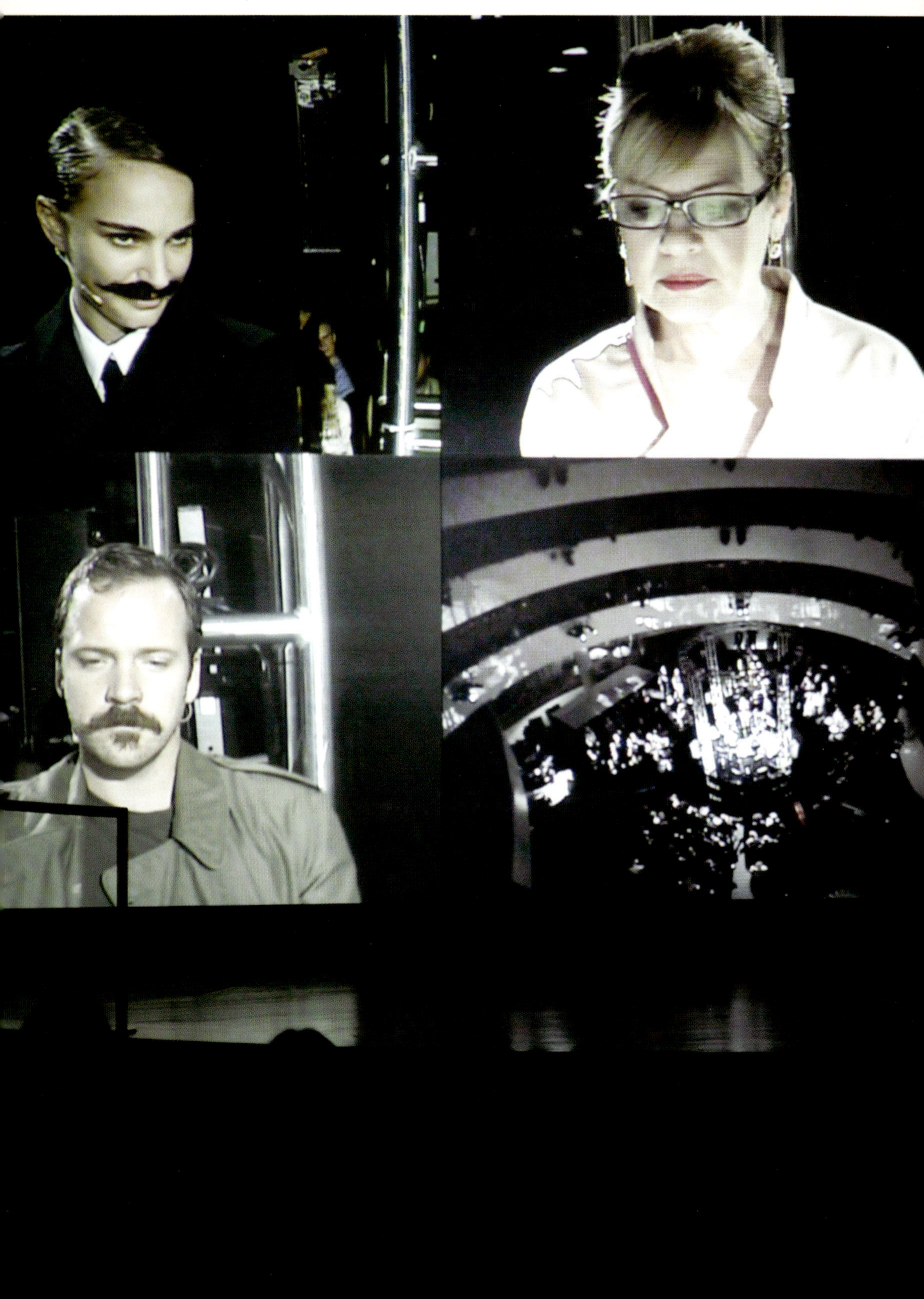

LAUDISI: HOW CAN YOU BE SURE? MY BET IS WE'LL SEE A GHOST. ANOTHER FRAGMENT.

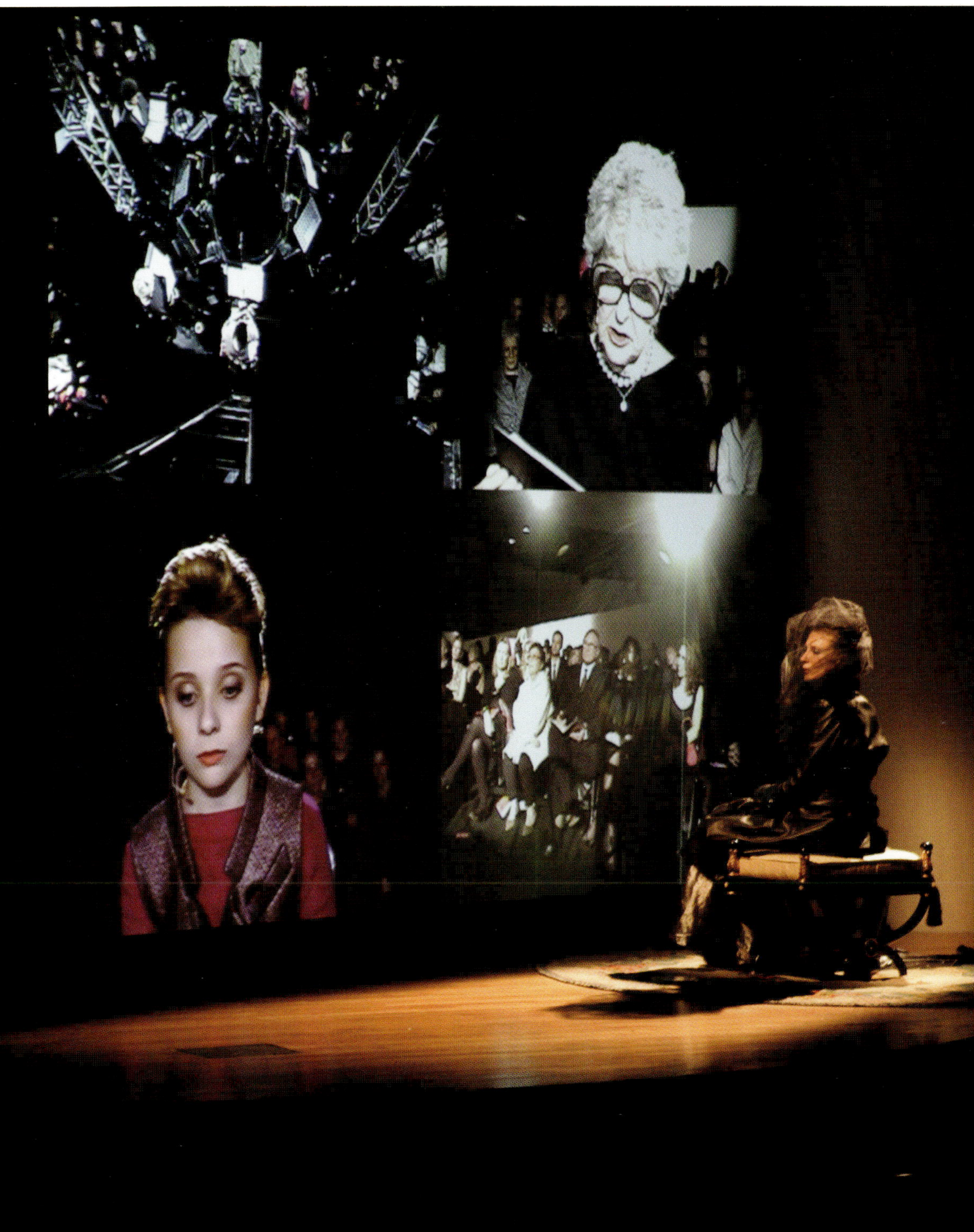

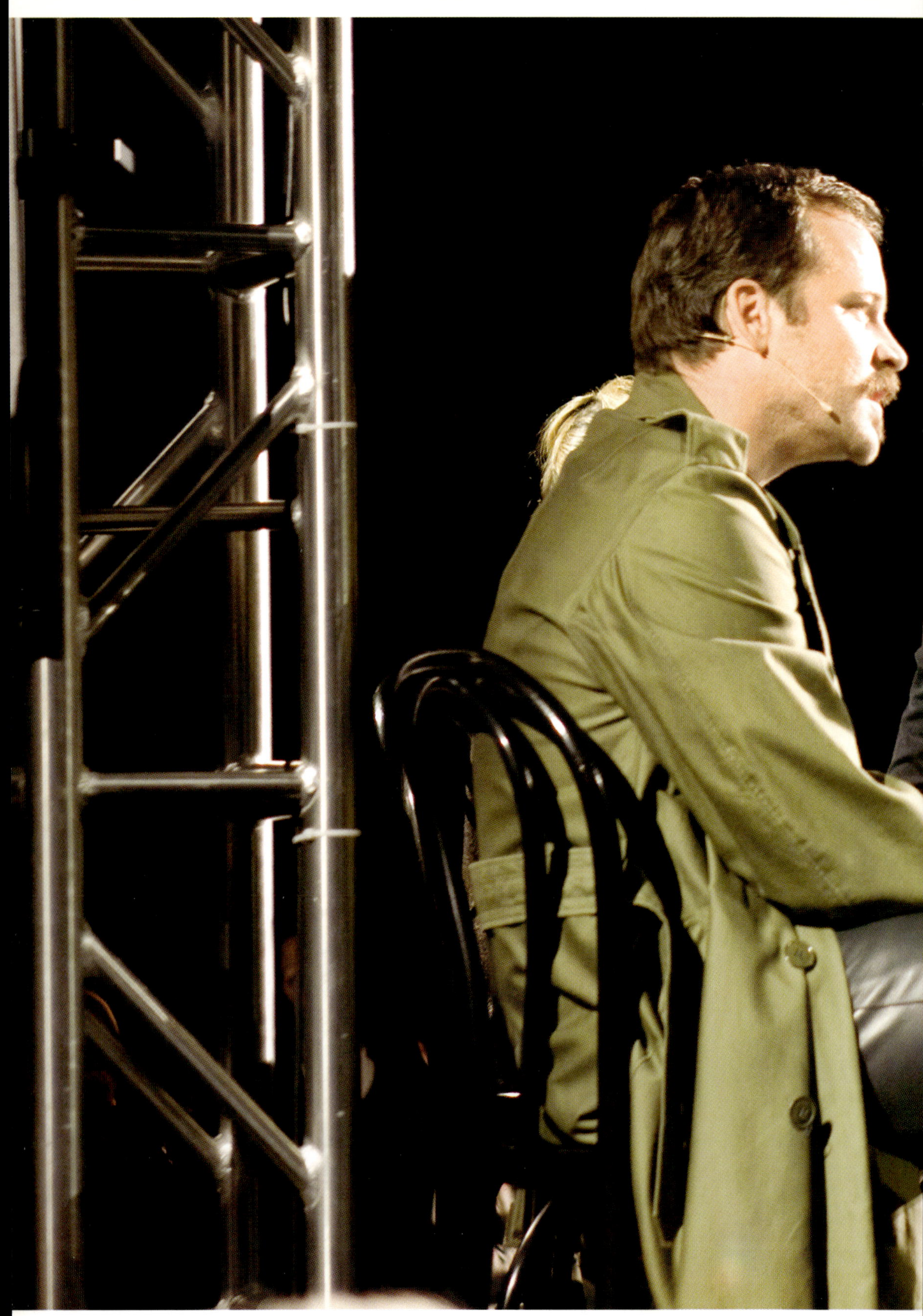
AGAZZI: A GHOST. RIDICULOUS.

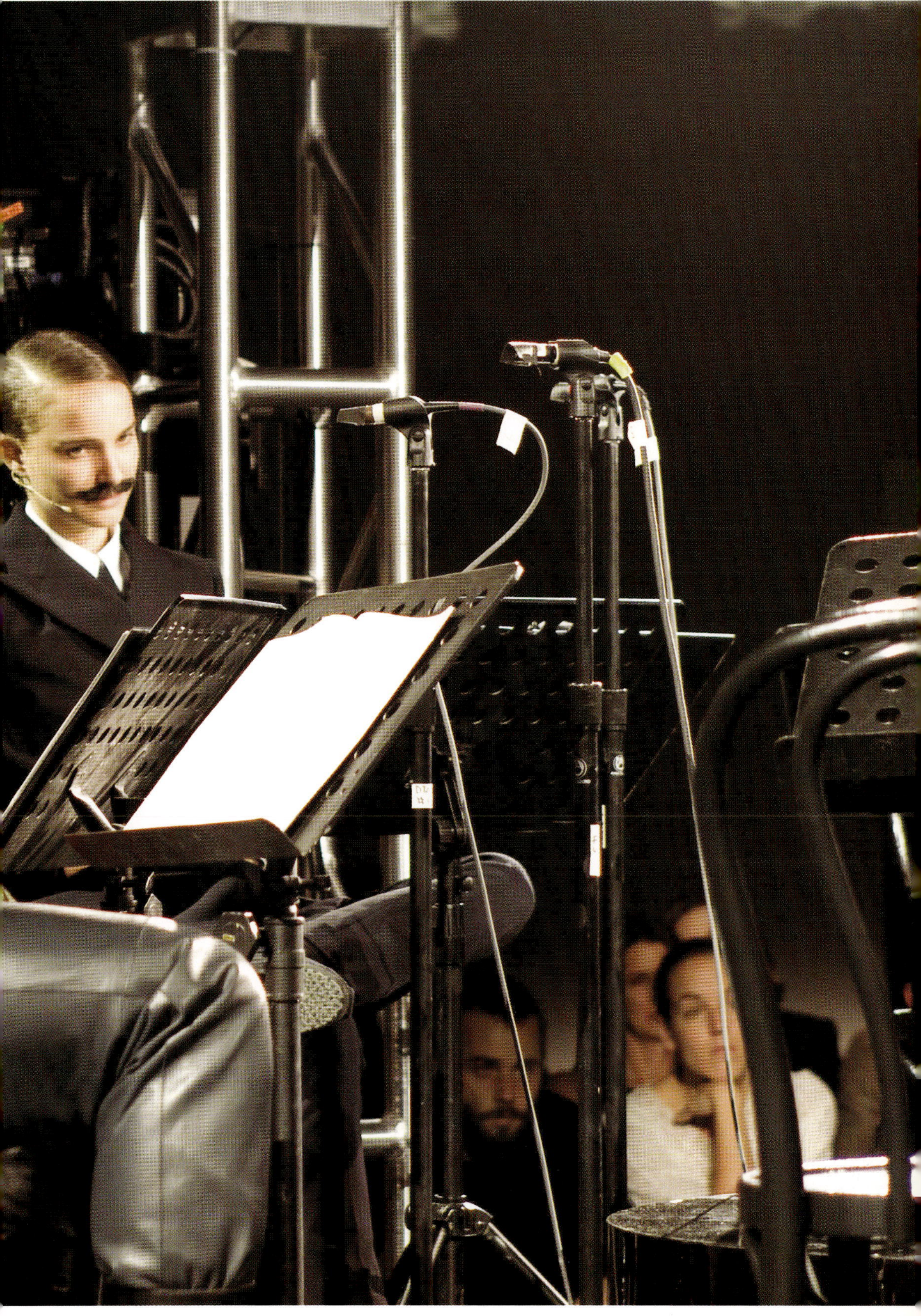

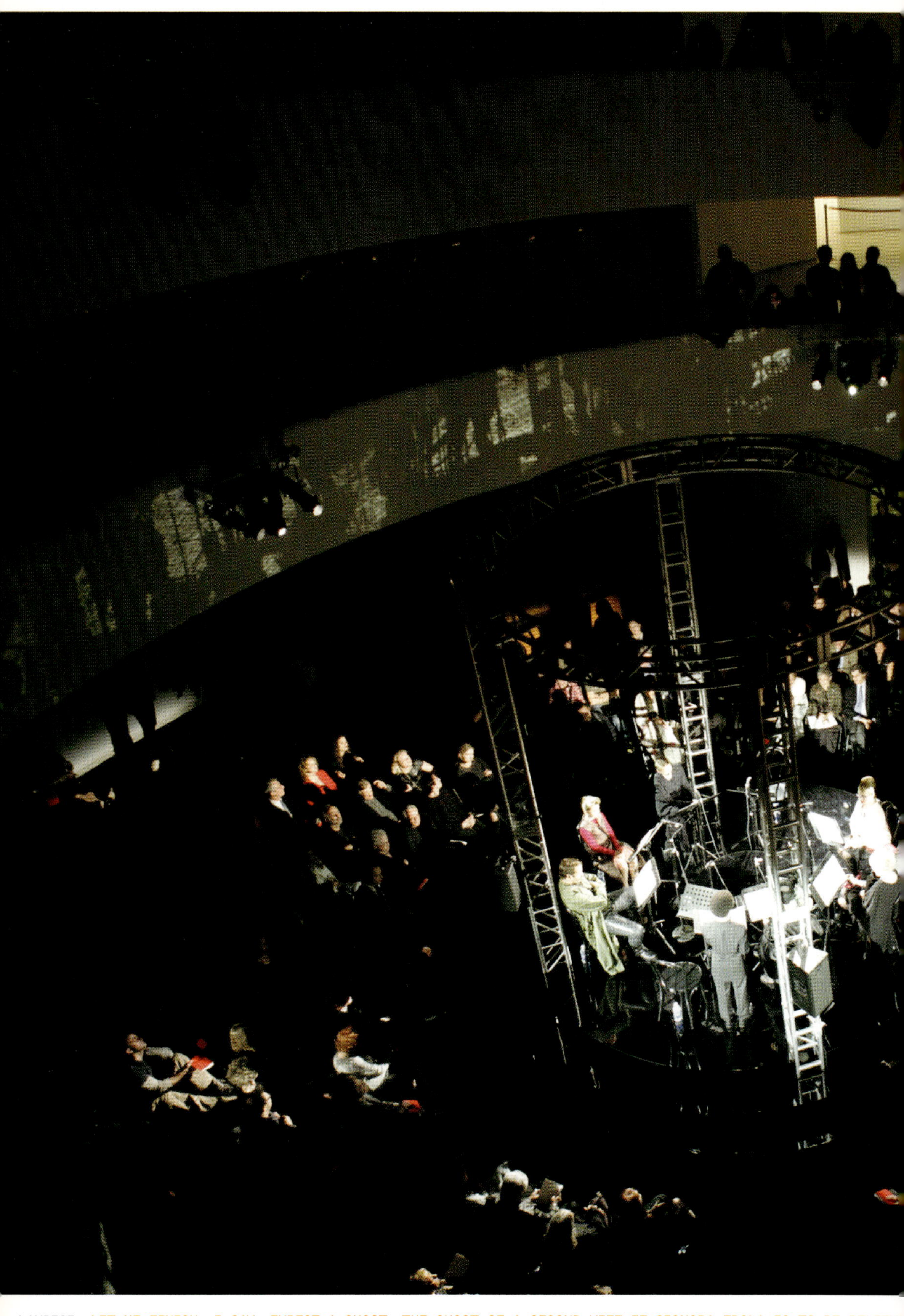

LAUDISI: LET ME FINISH. I SAY: EXPECT A GHOST. THE GHOST OF A SECOND WIFE IF SIGNORA FROLA IS TO BE BELIEV

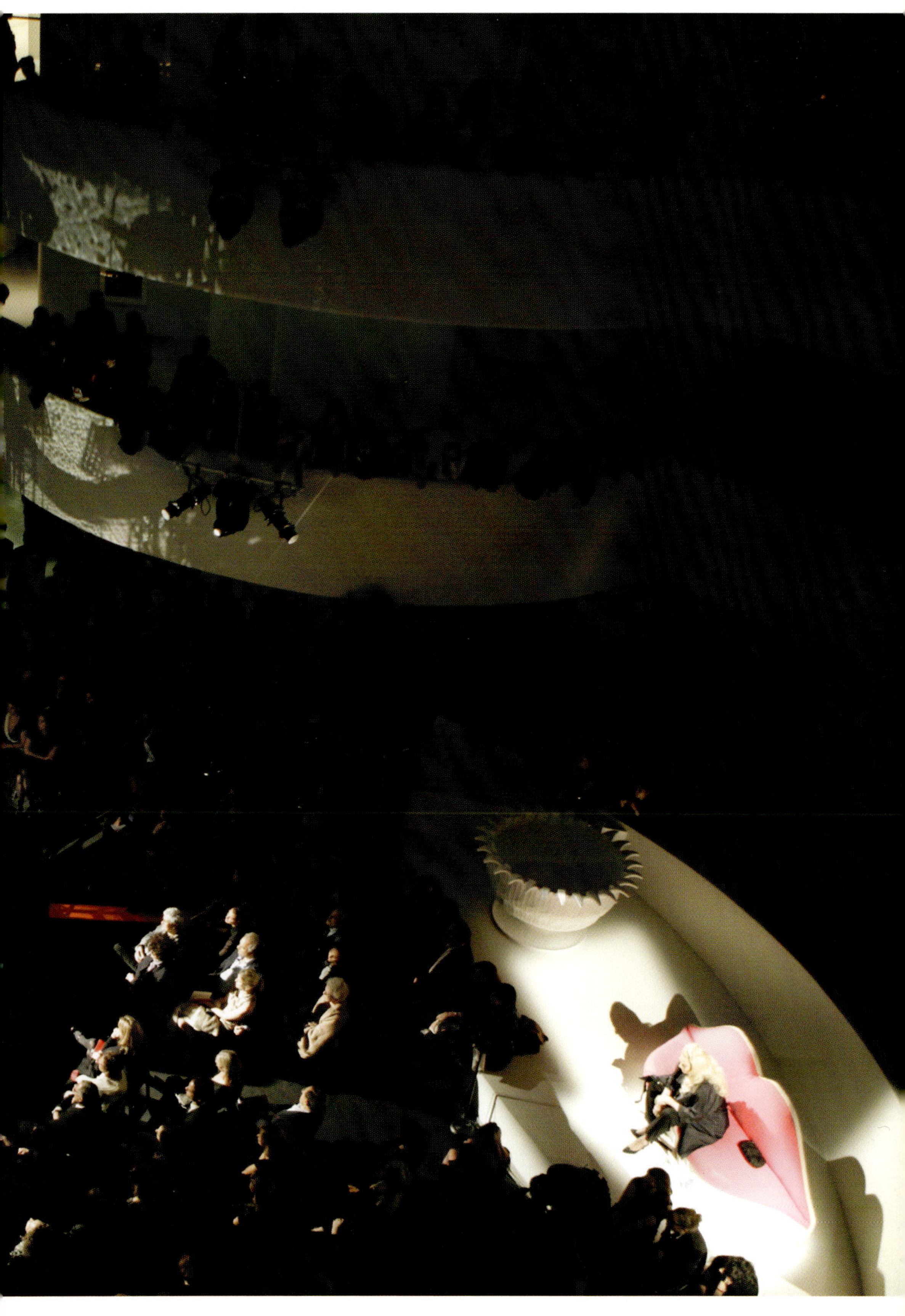

ND THE GHOST OF A DAUGHTER IF SIGNOR PONZA IS RIGHT. I CAN'T SEE HOW YOU COULD EXPECT ANYTHING ELSE.

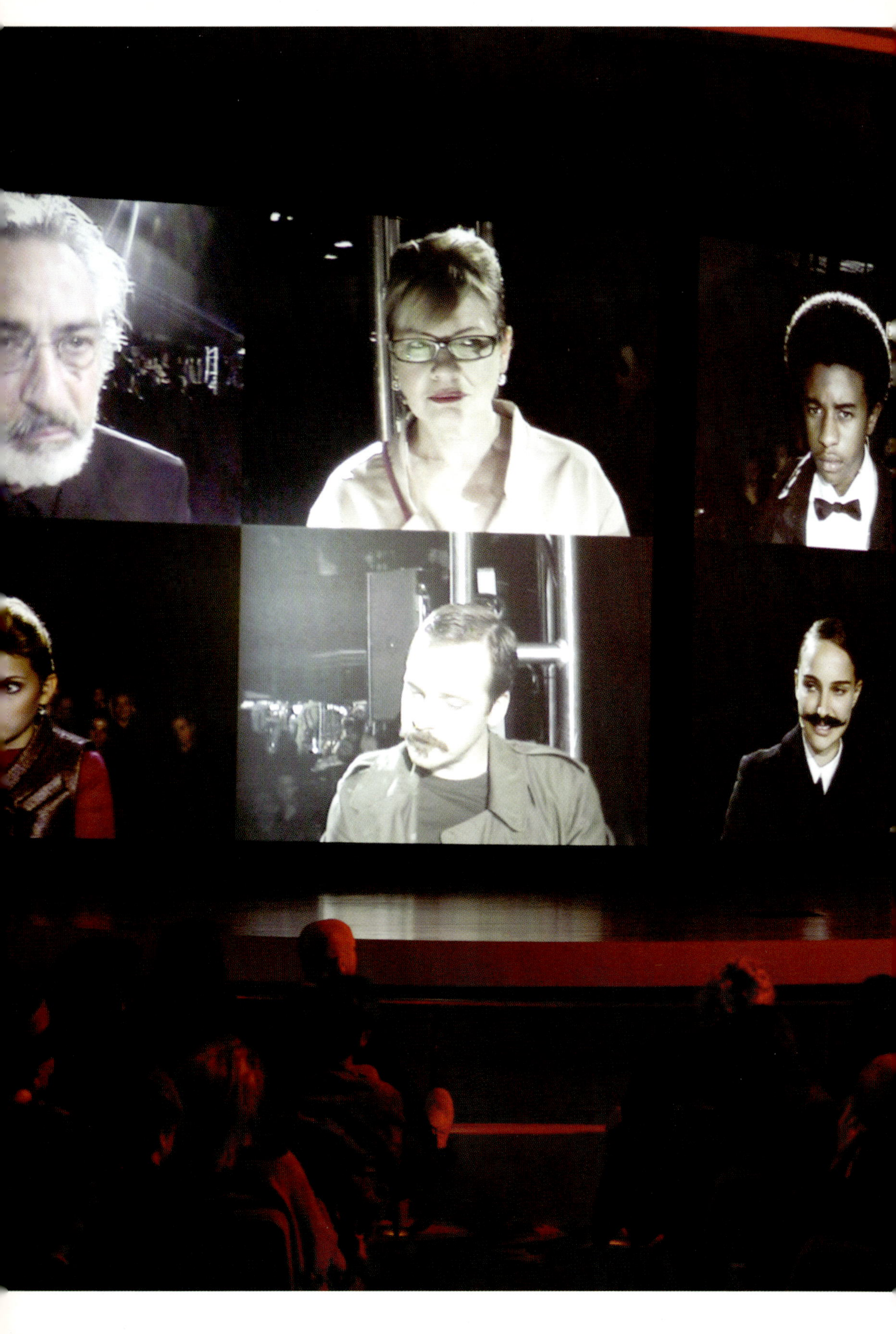

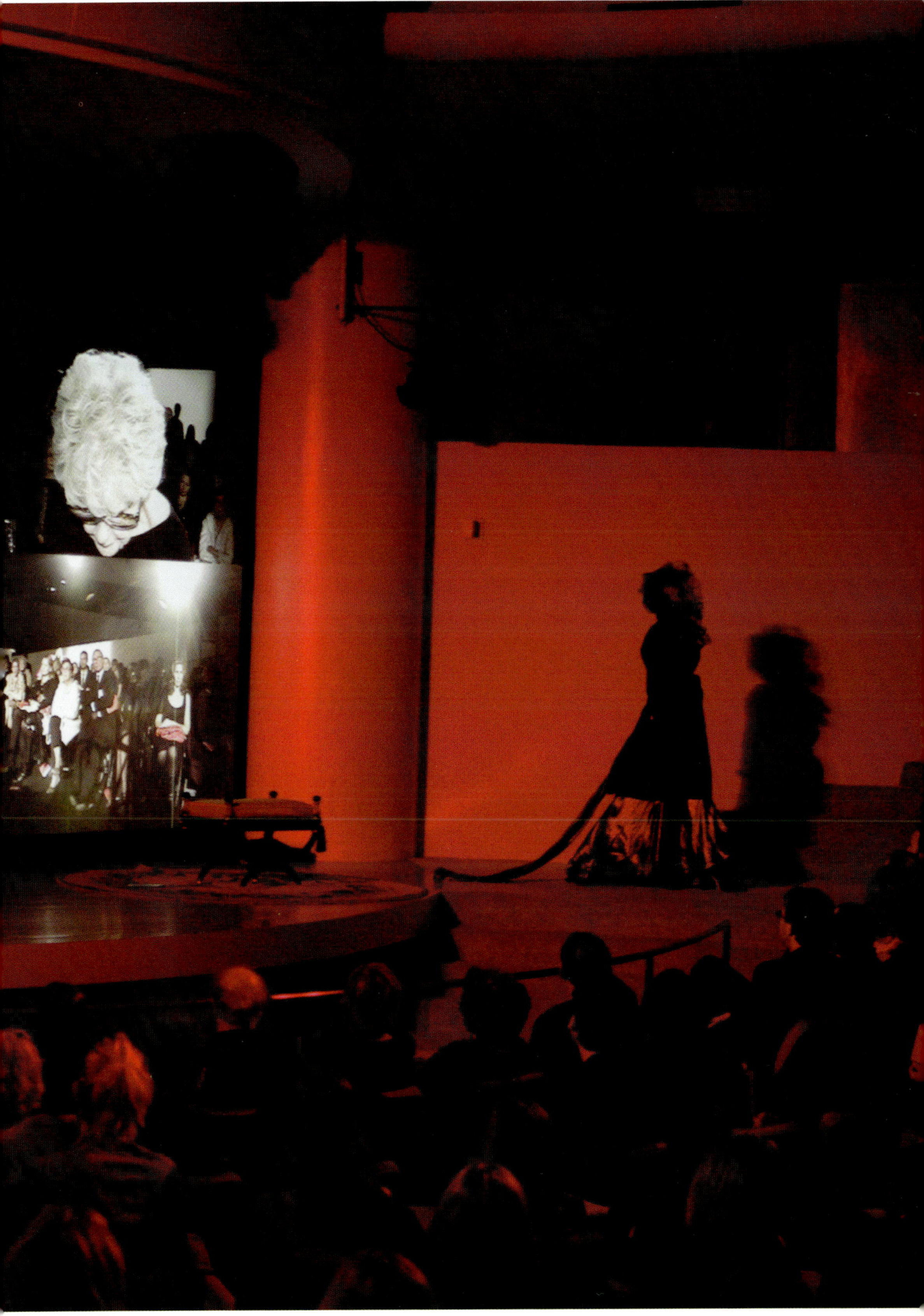

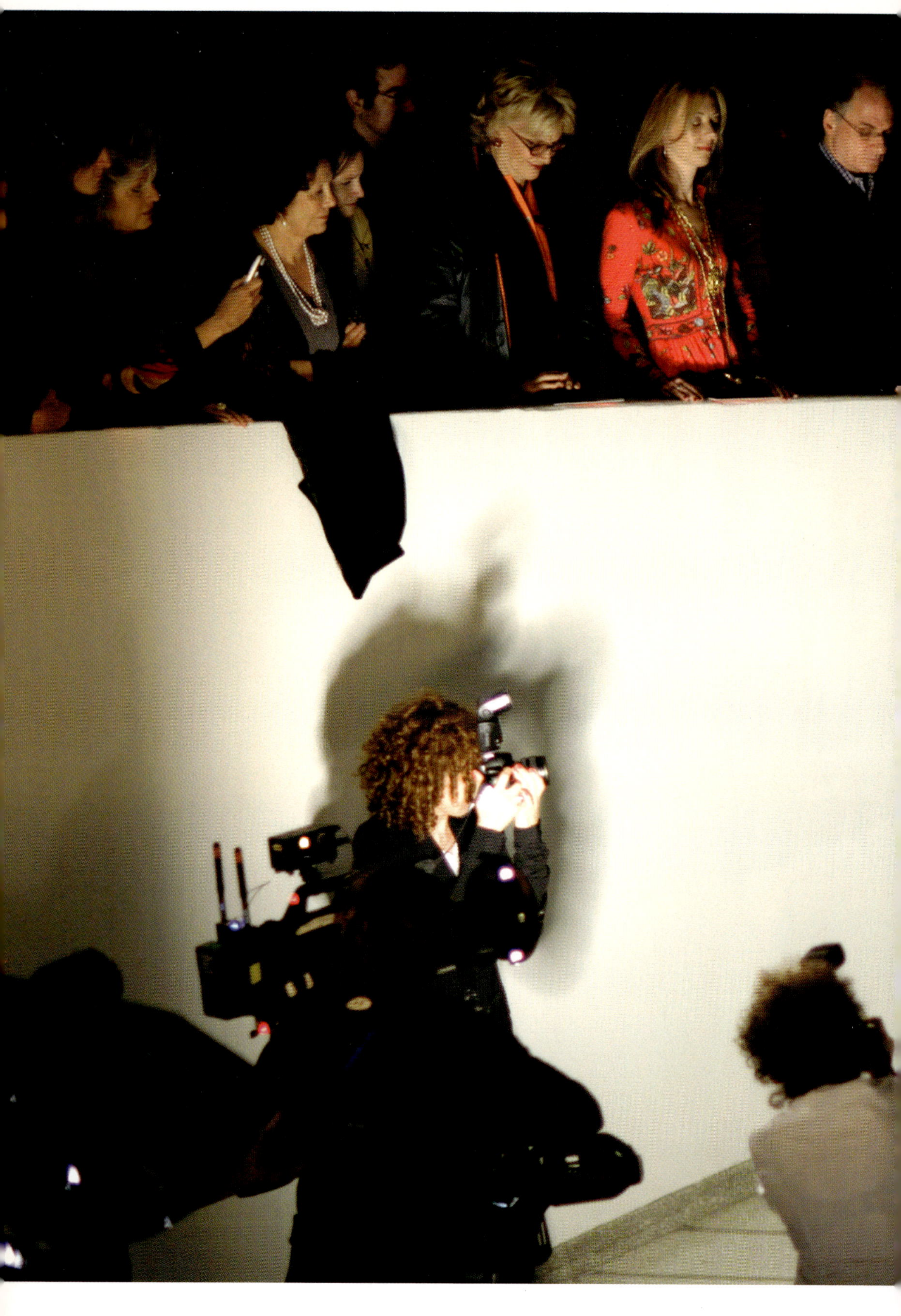

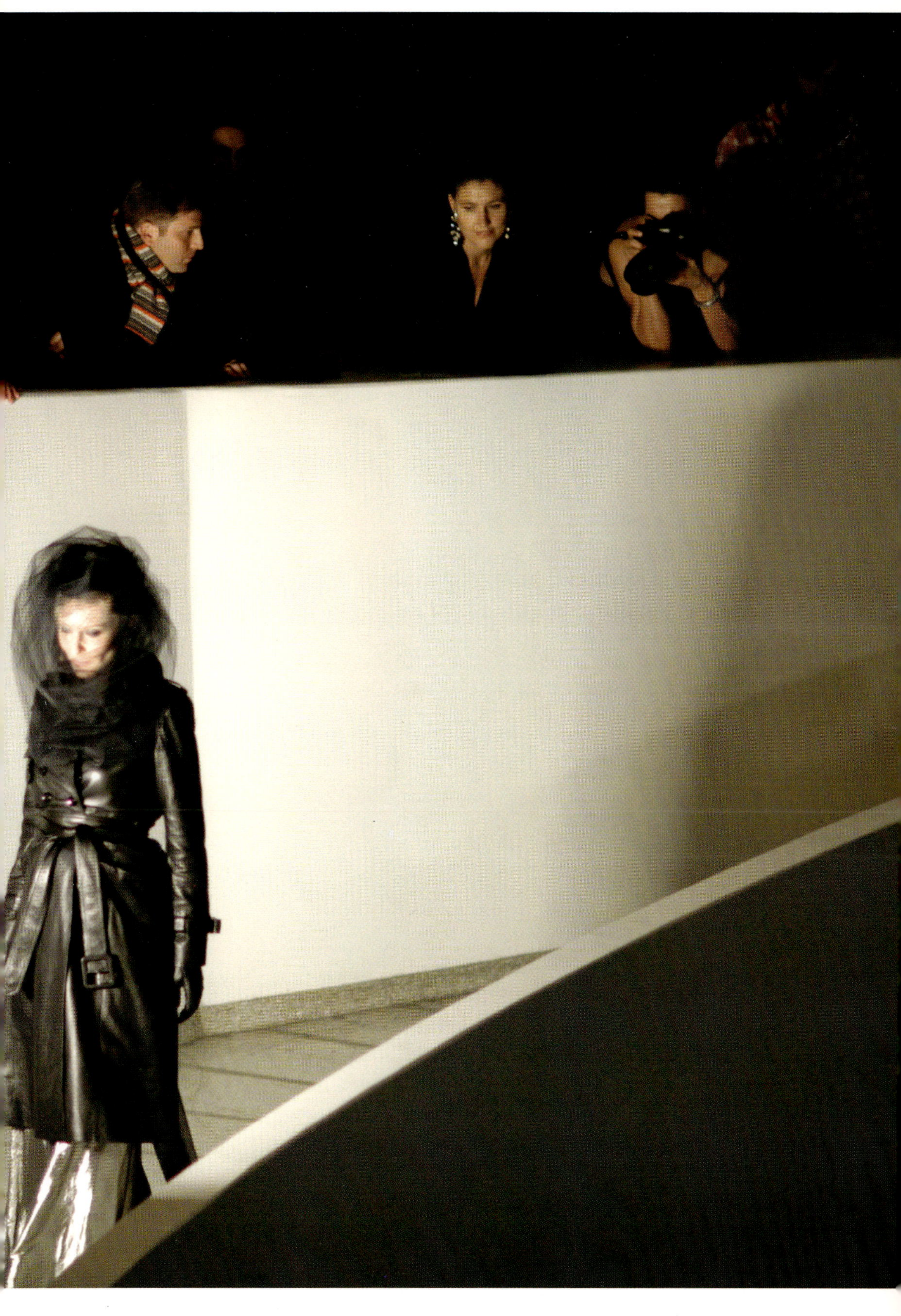

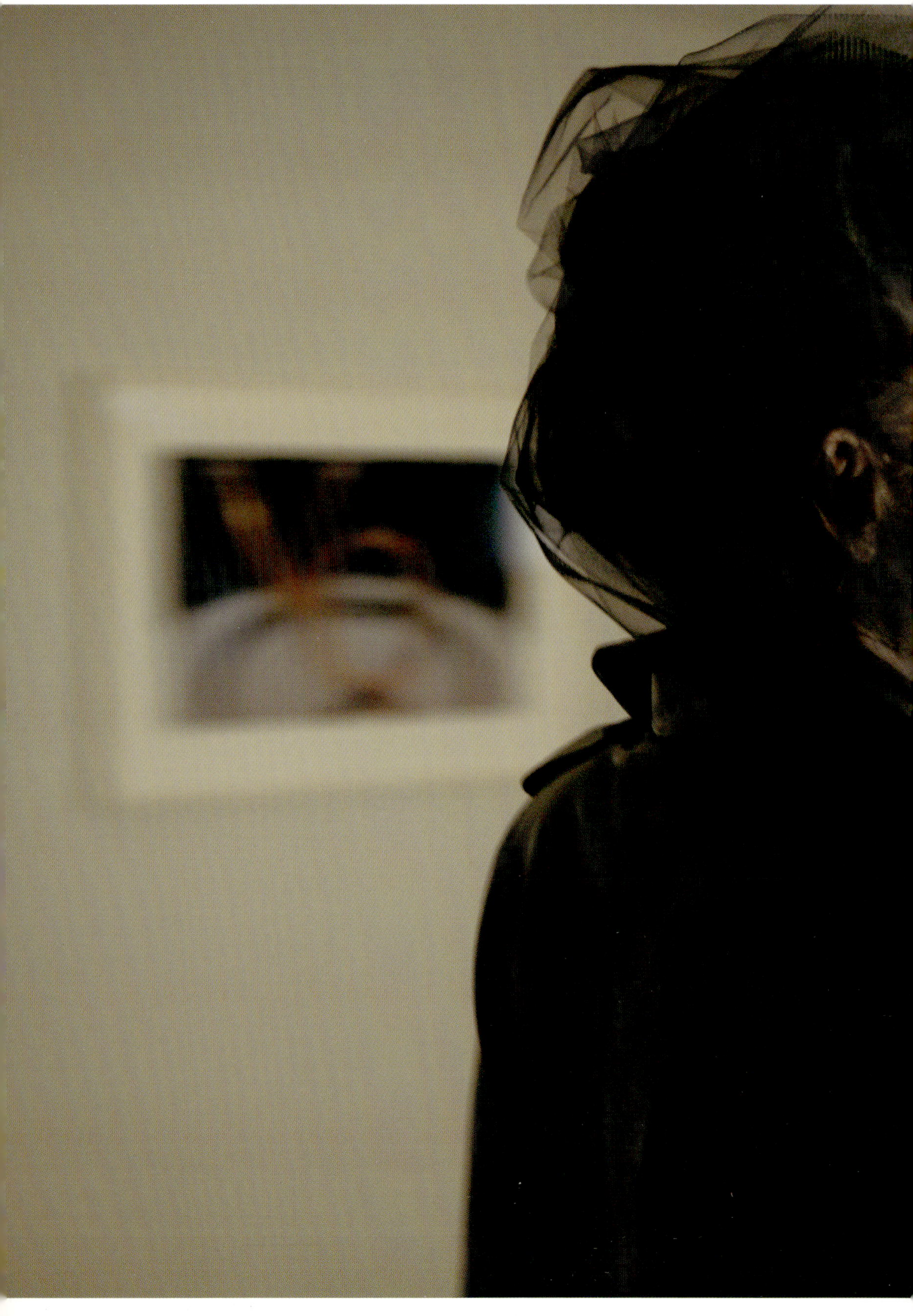

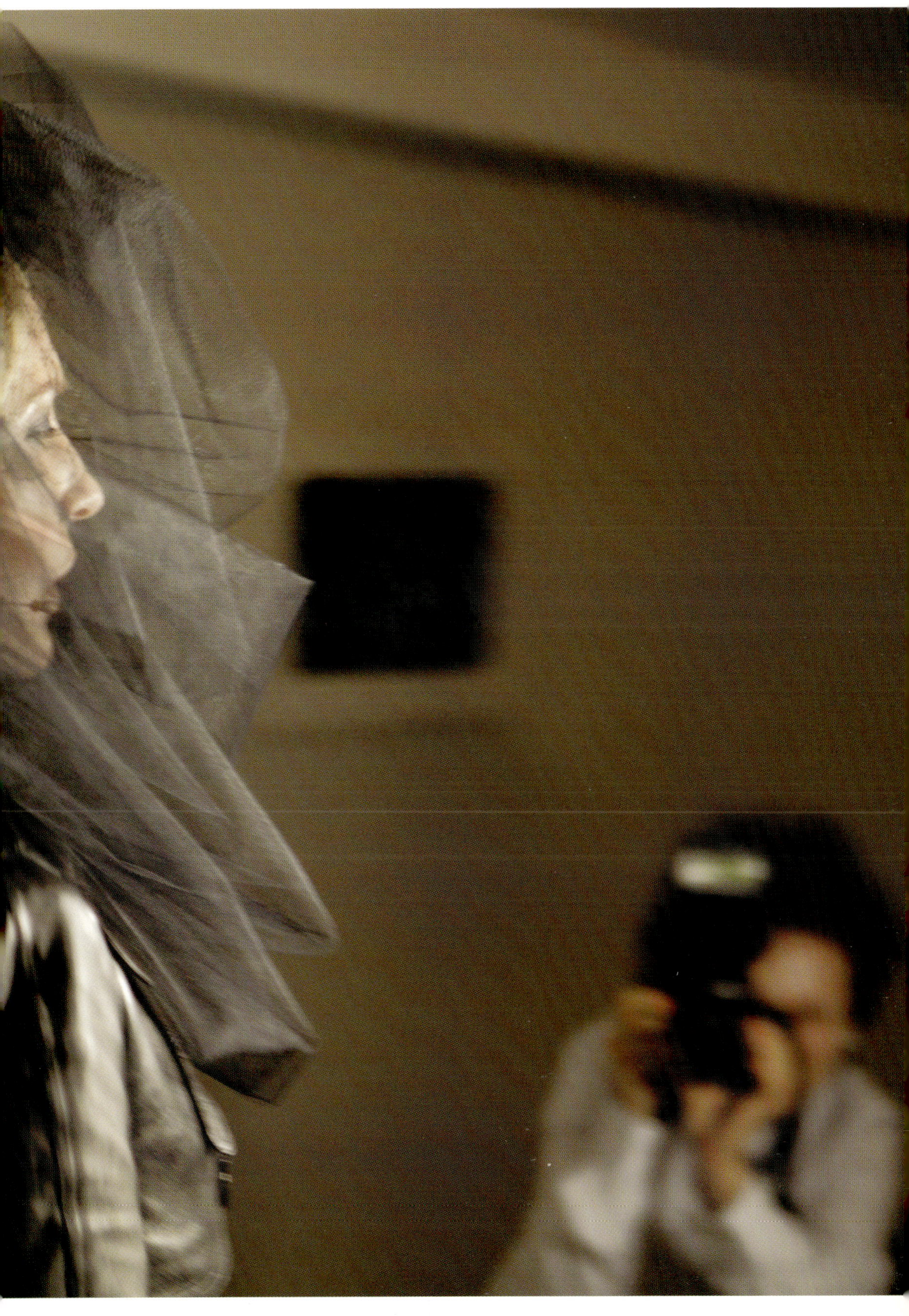

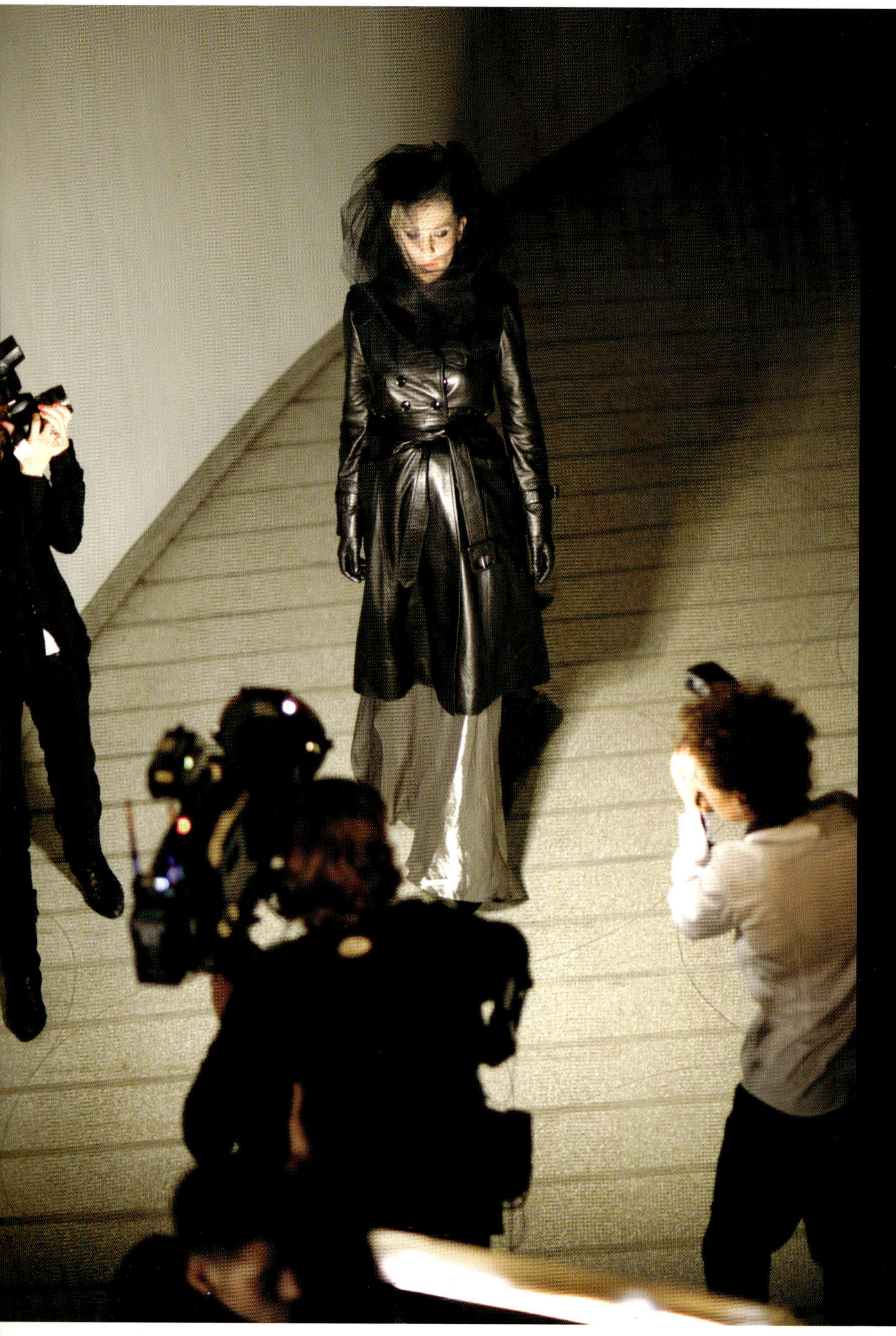

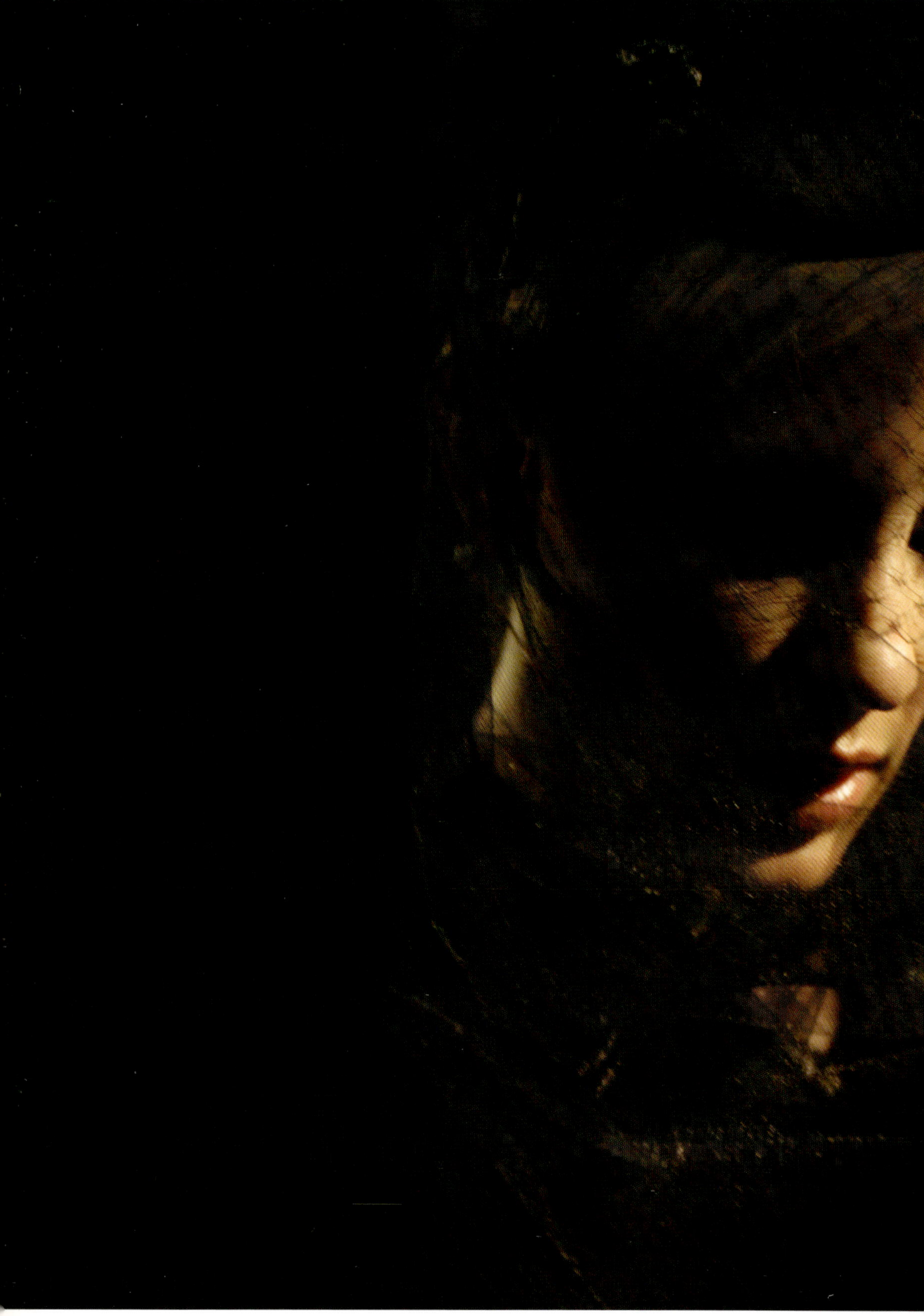

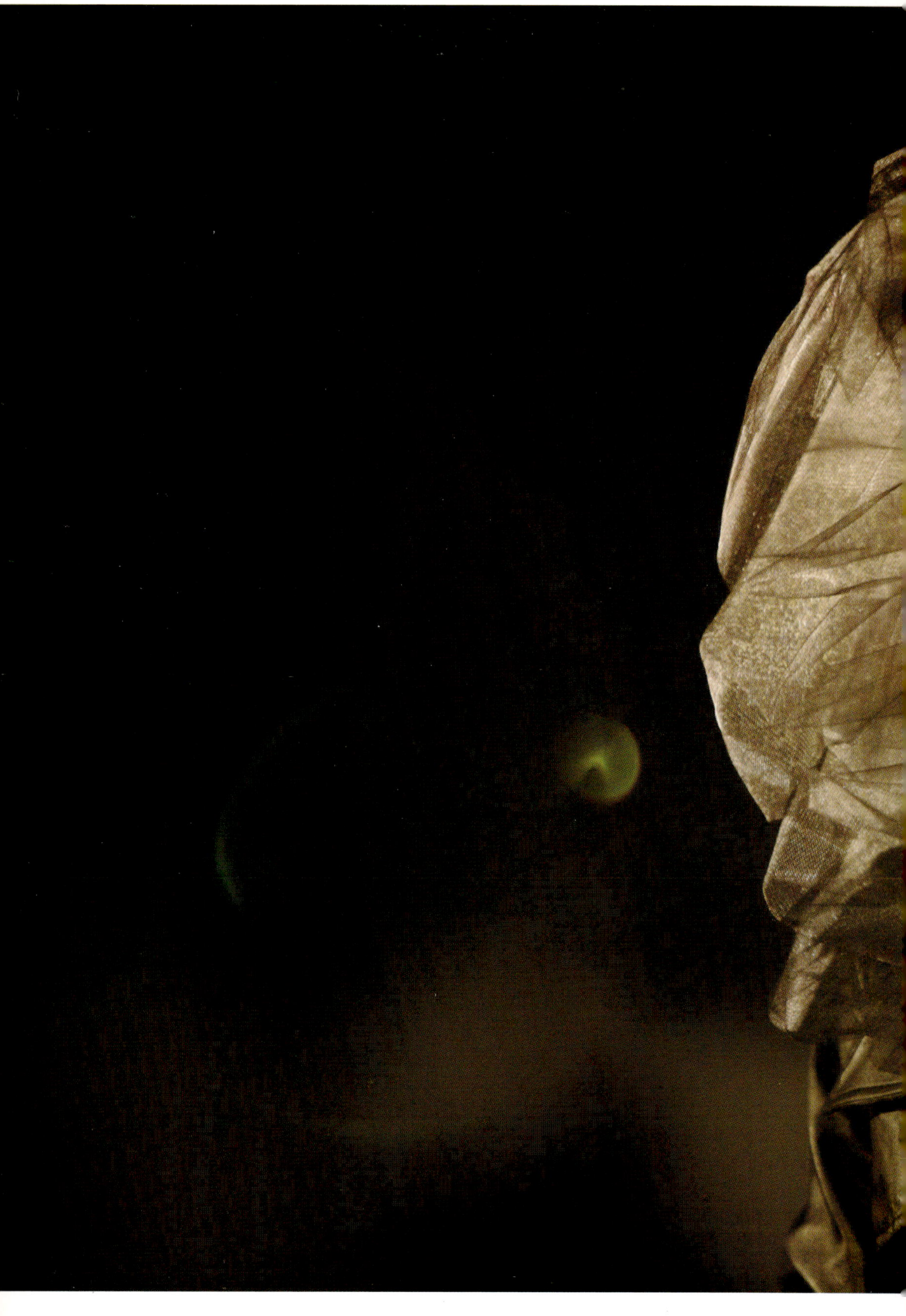

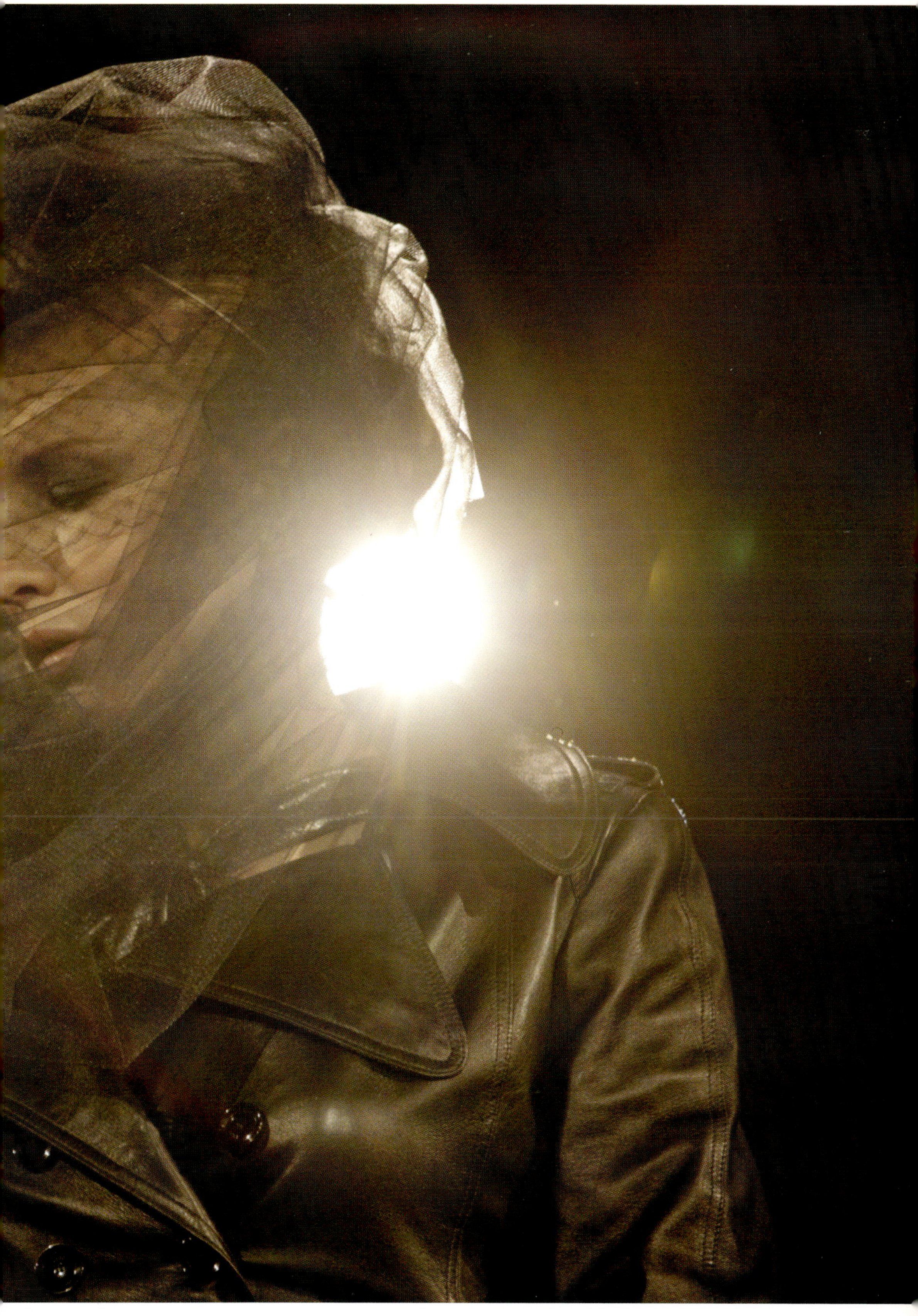

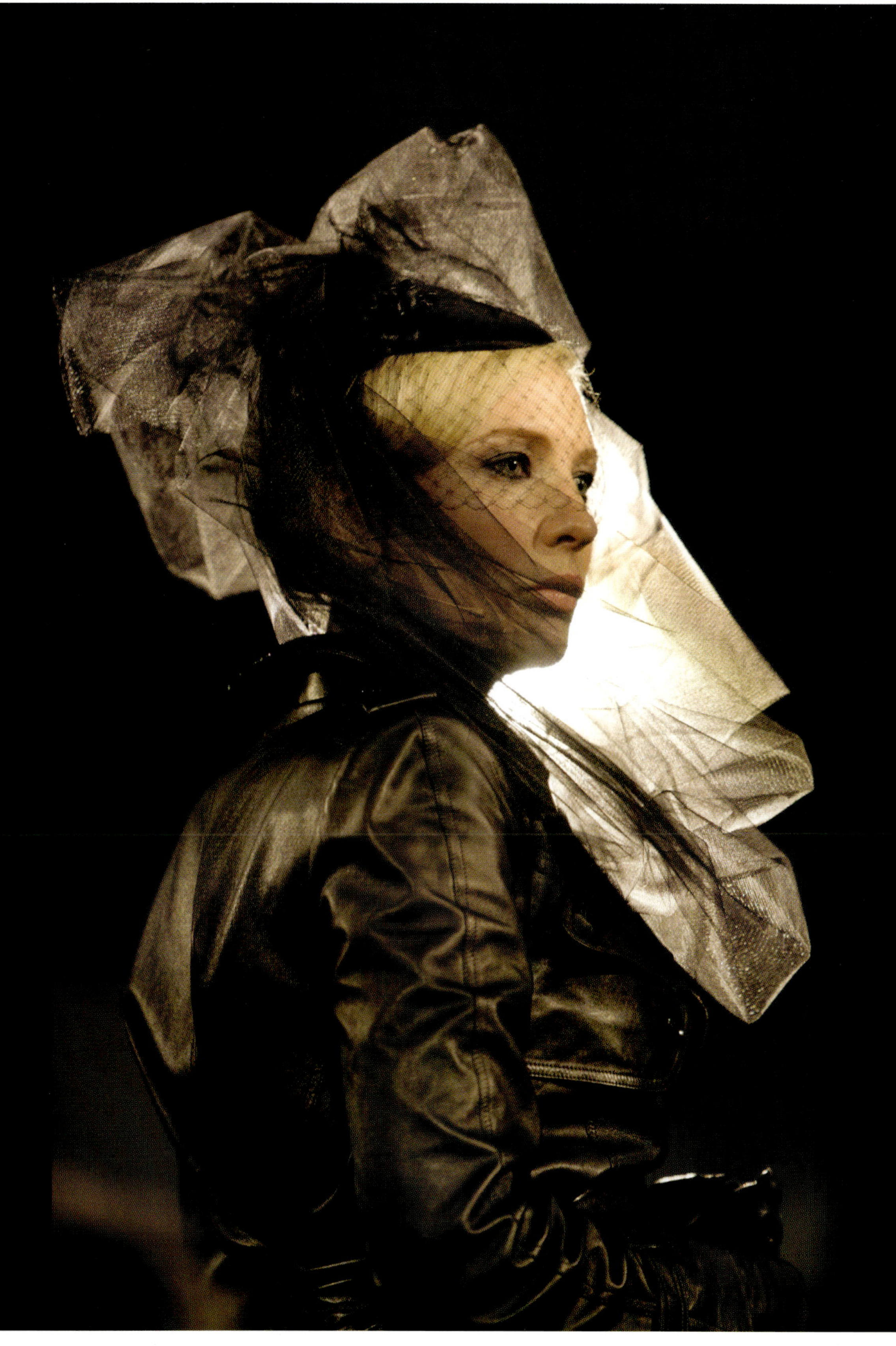

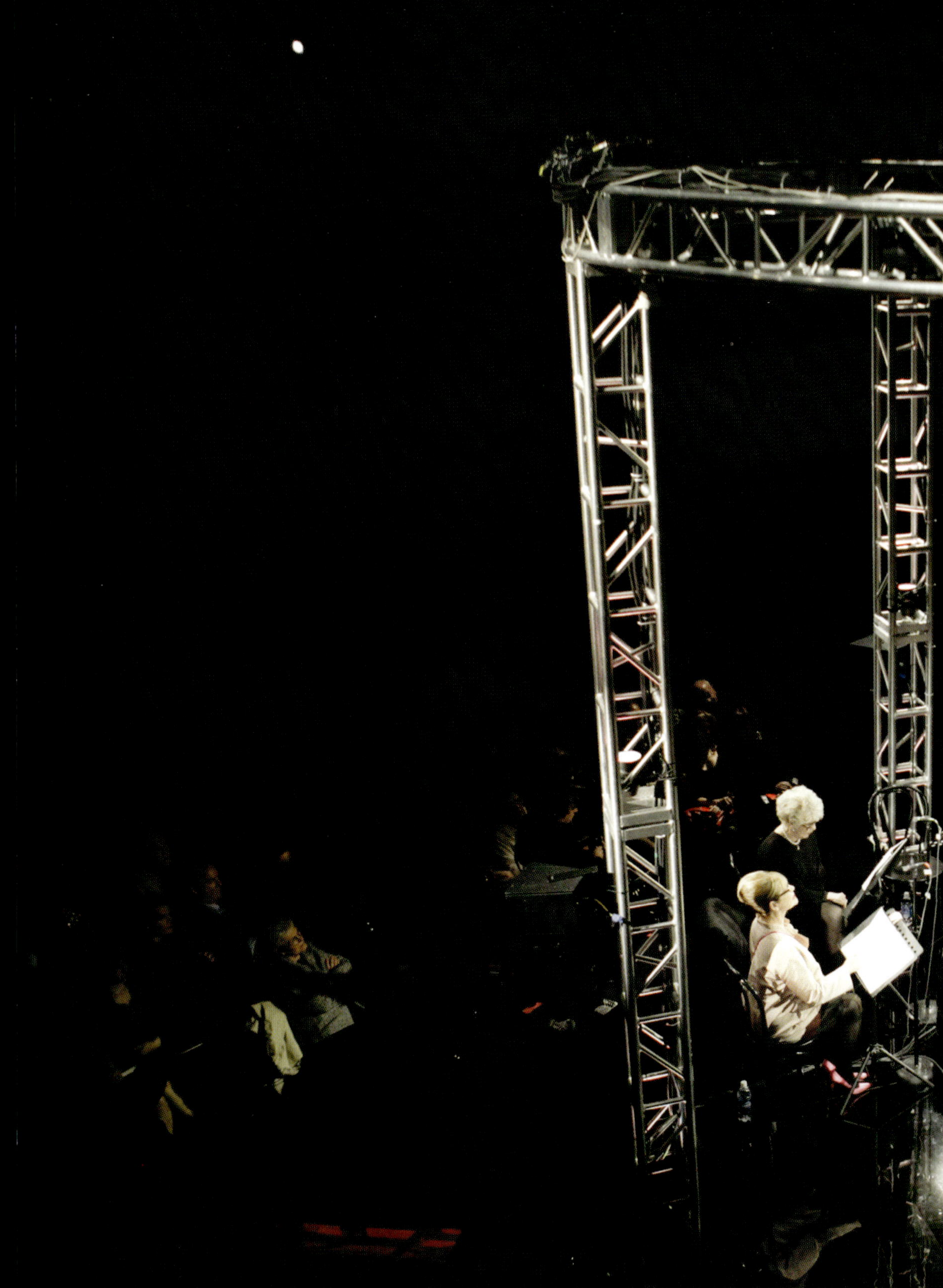

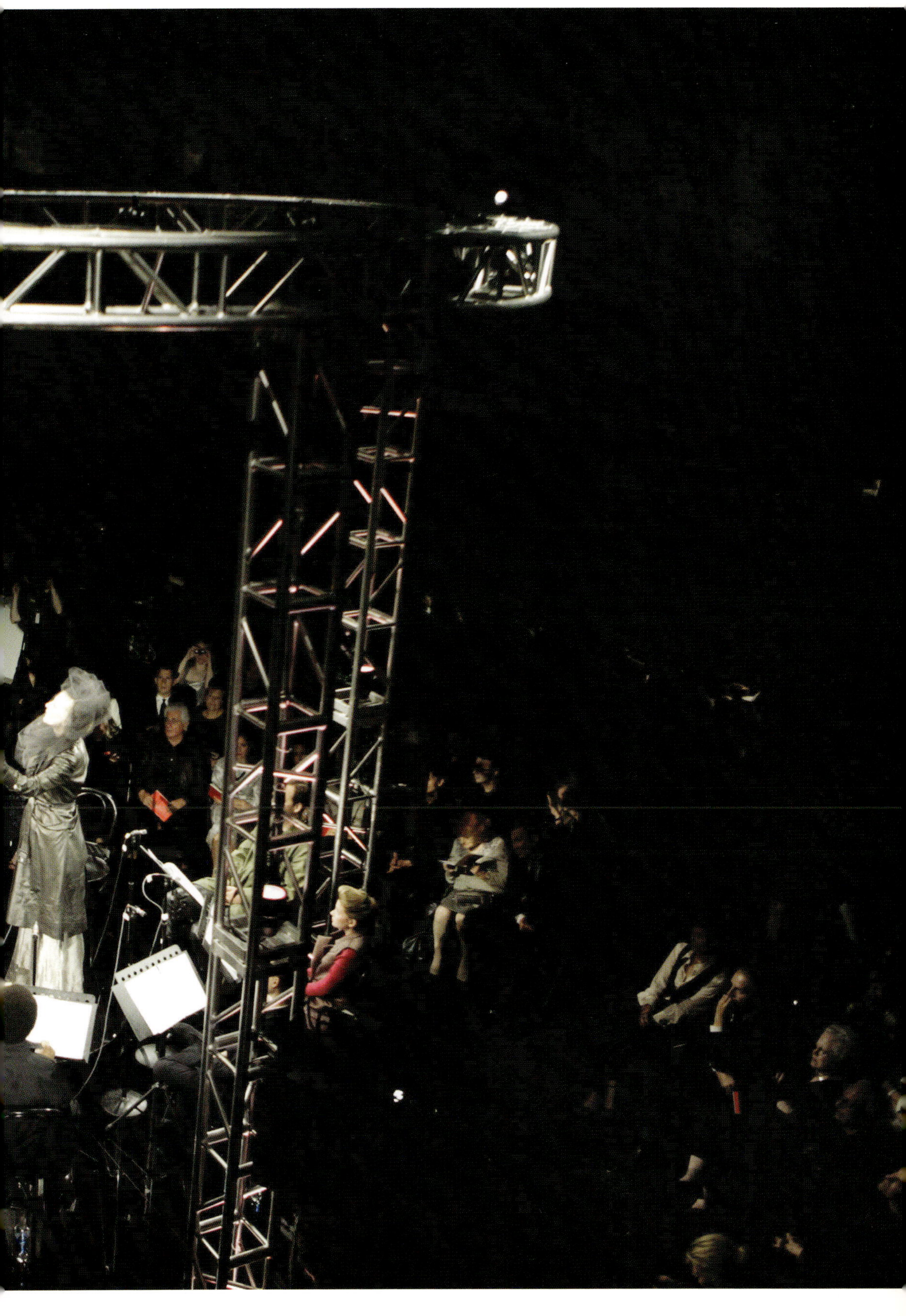

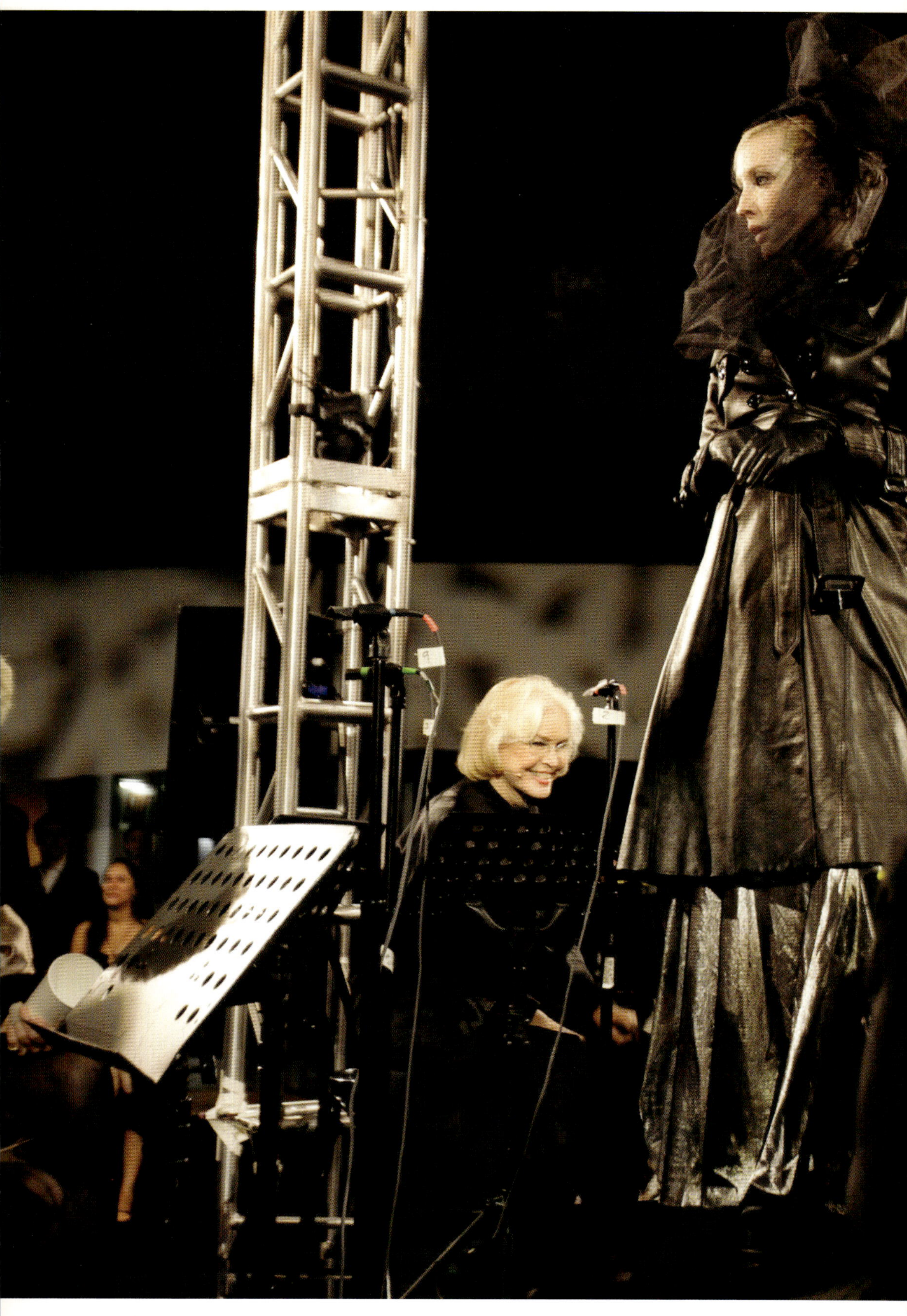

SIGNORA PONZA: TELL YOU WHAT? THE TRUTH? THE TRUTH IS SIMPLY THIS: I AM SIGNORA FROLA'S DAUGHTER

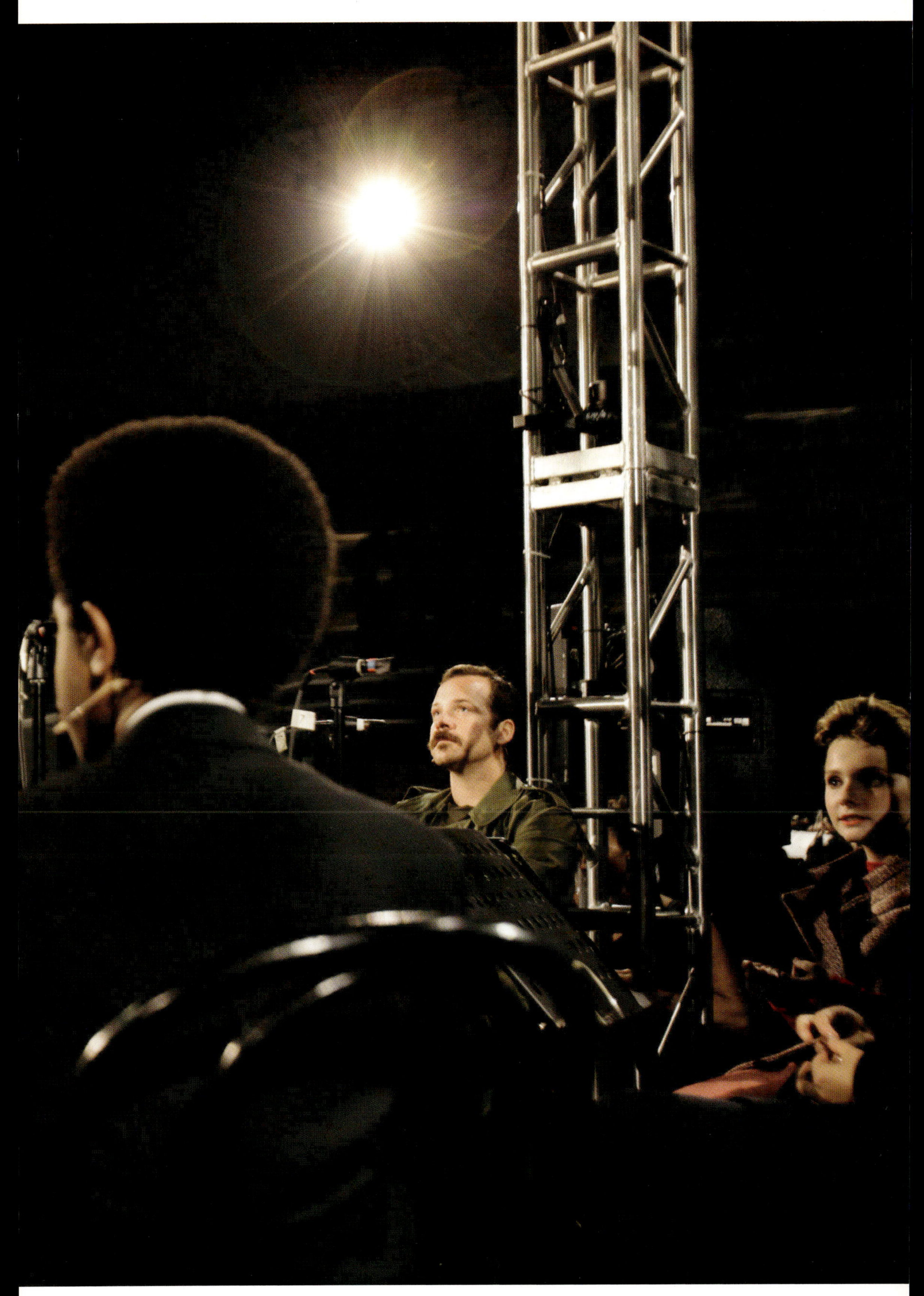

AND. I AM SIGNOR PONZA'S SECOND WIFE. I AM BOTH AND — ALONE. IN MY TOWER — I AM NOBODY.

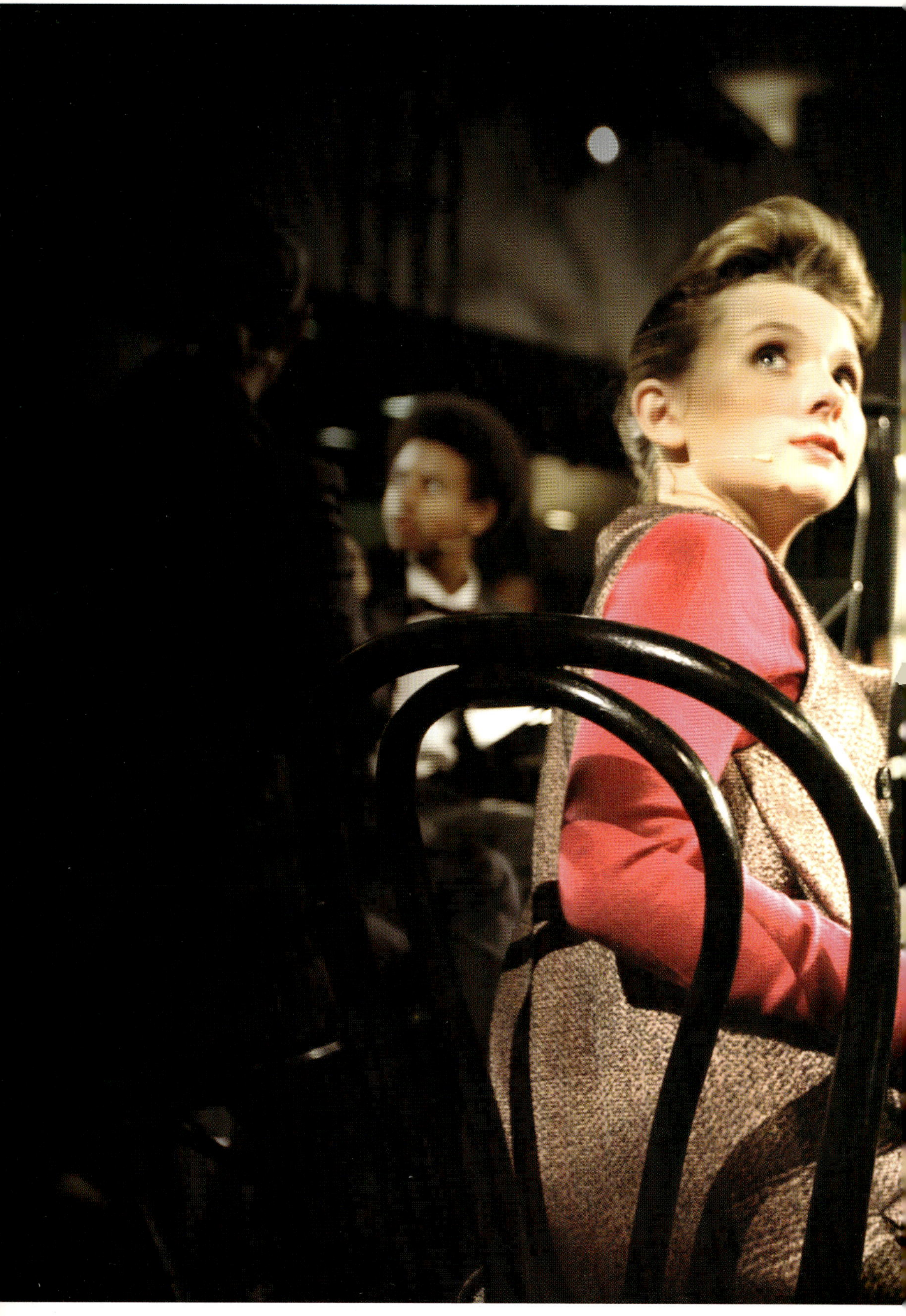

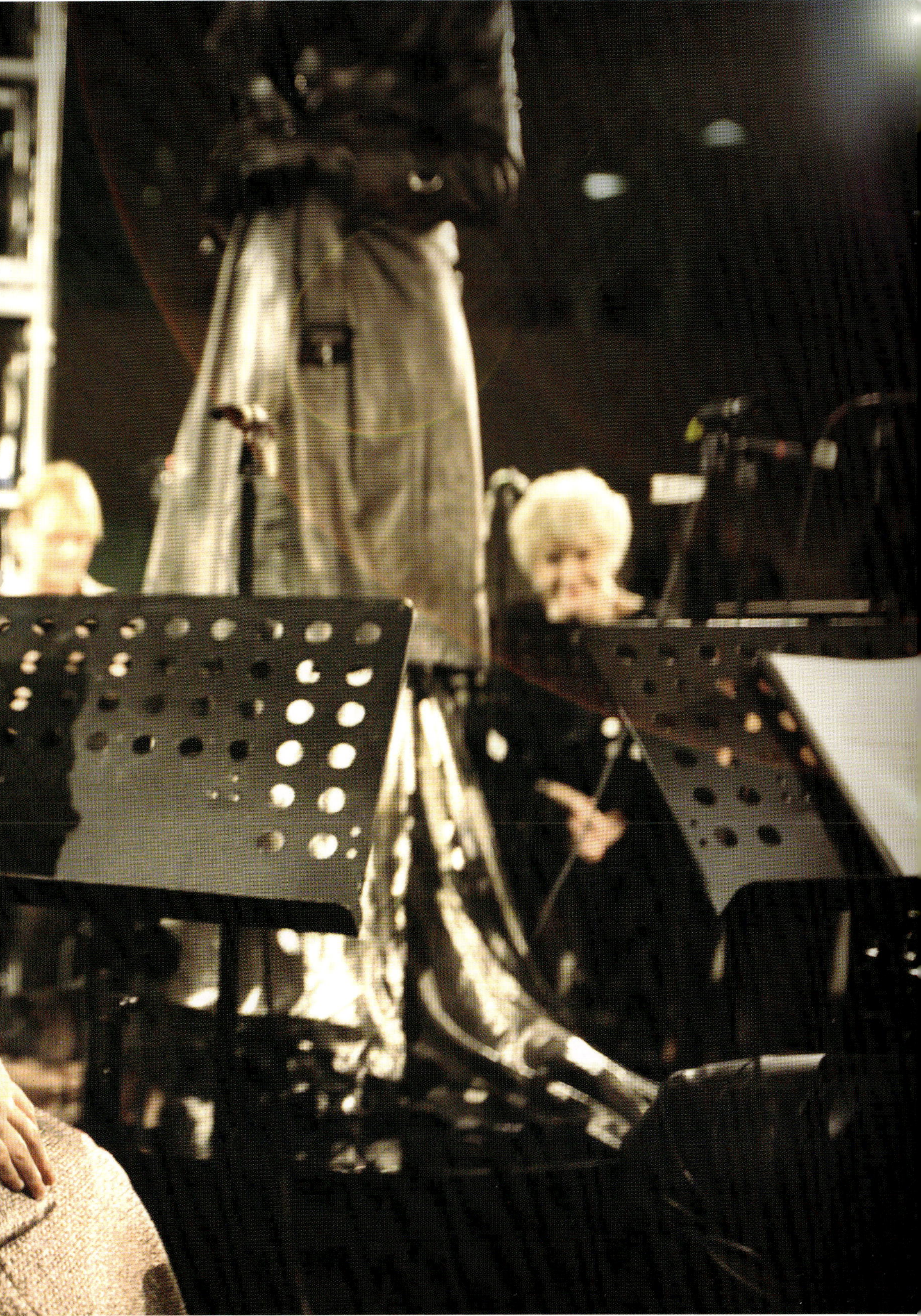

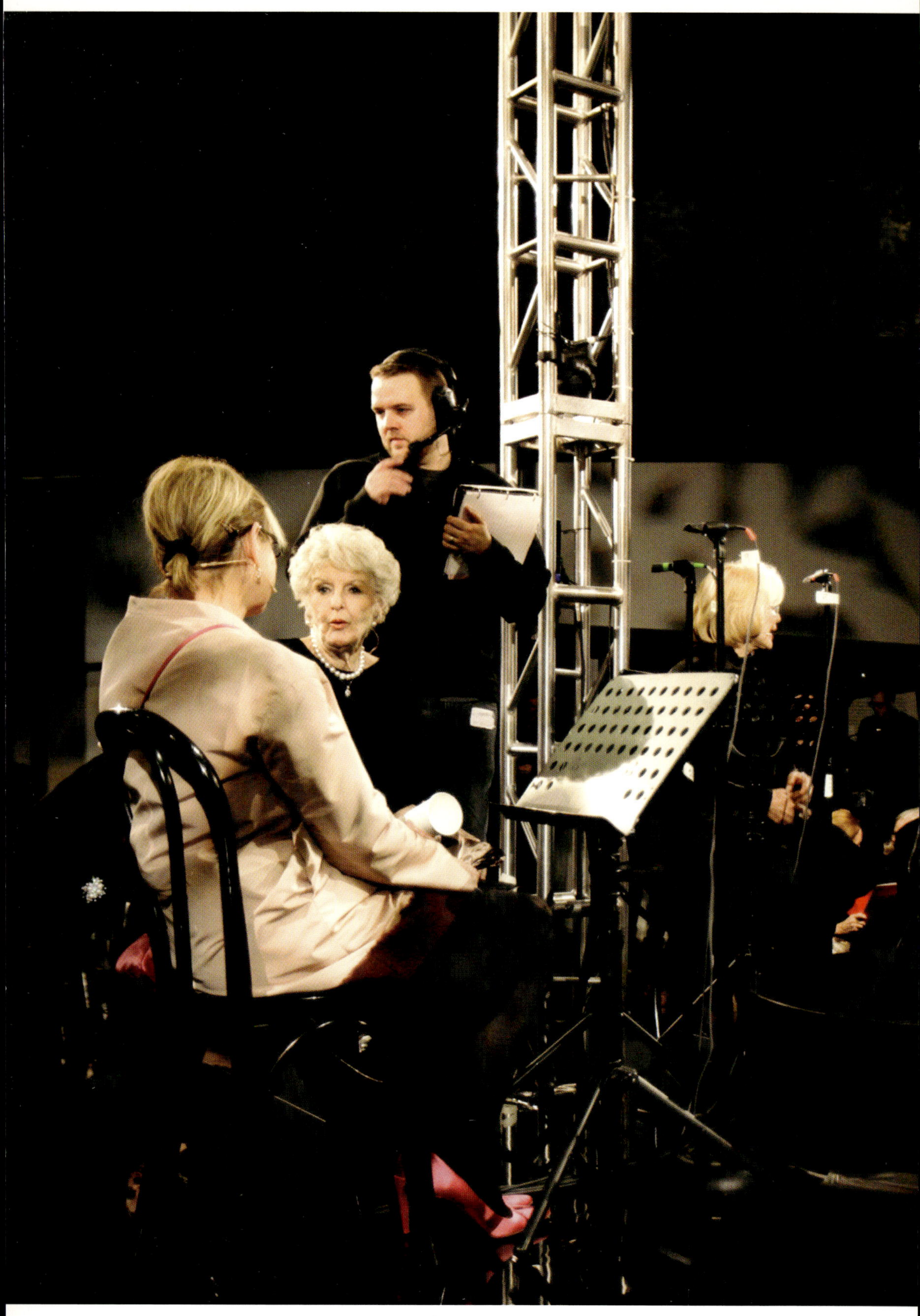

AMALIA AGAZZI: BUT REALLY SIGNORA...REALLY. NO, YOU ARE ONE OR THE OTHER.

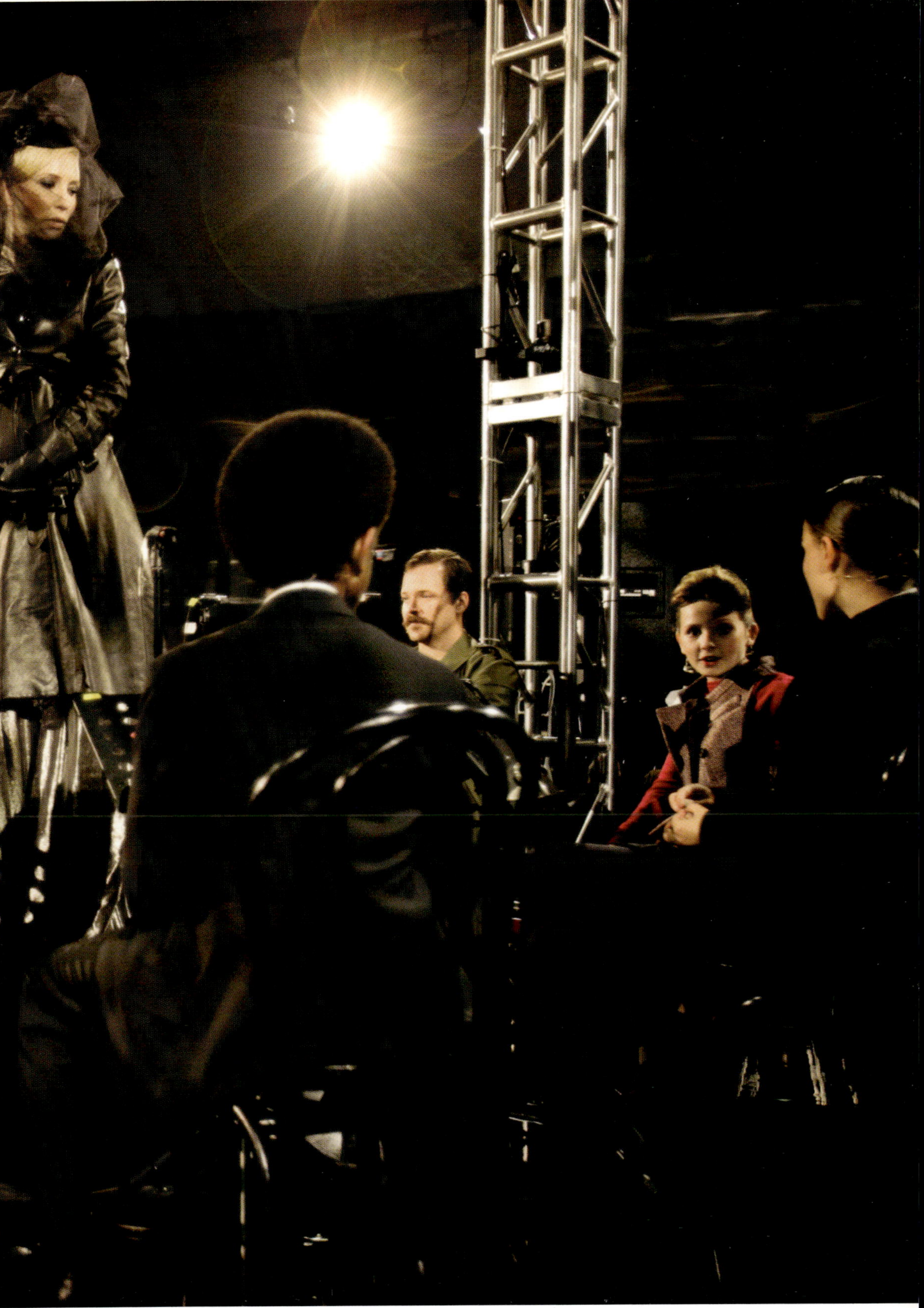

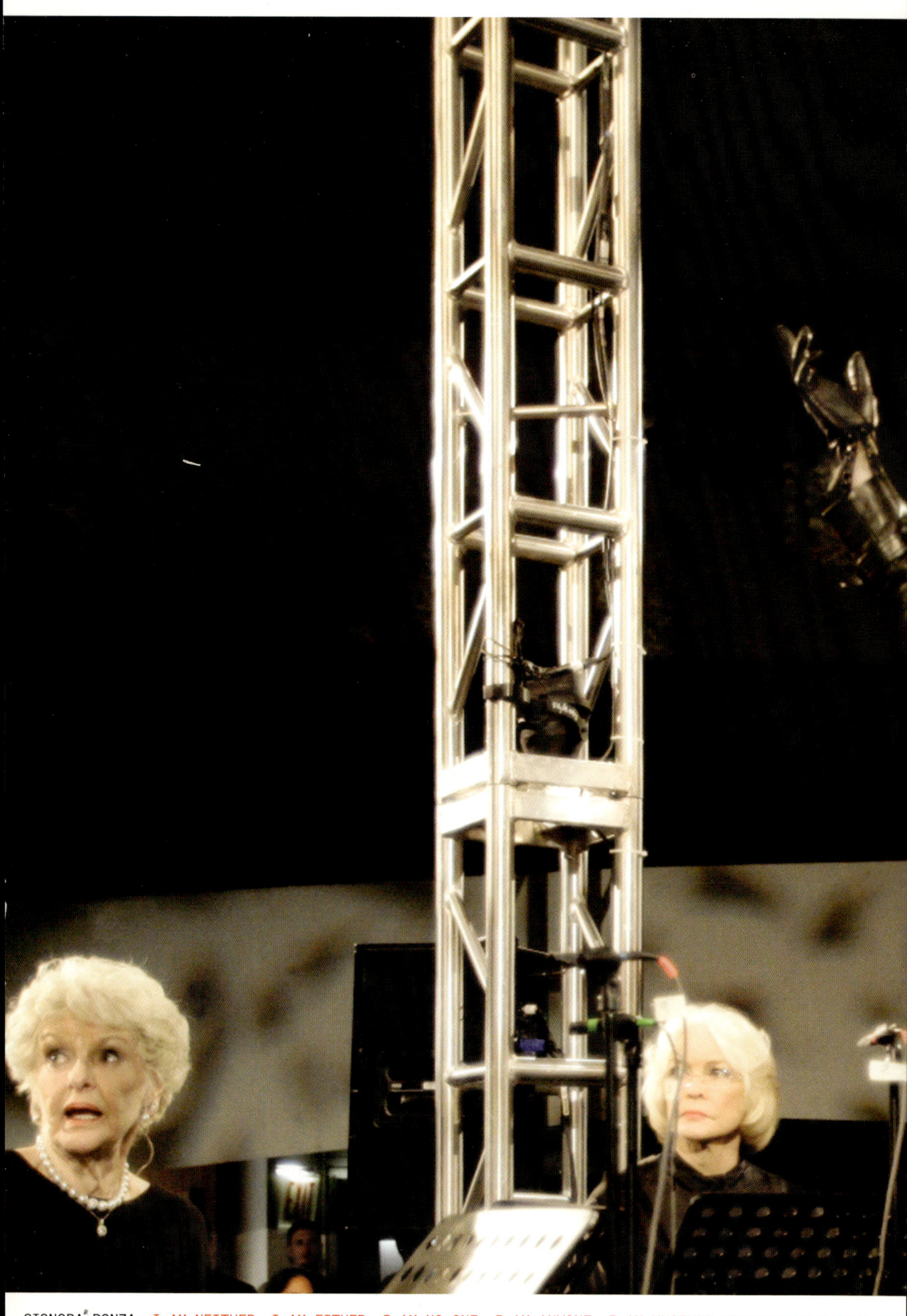

SIGNORA PONZA: I AM NEITHER, I AM EITHER, I AM NO ONE, I AM ANYONE. I AM WHOEVER YOU BELIEVE ME TO BE.

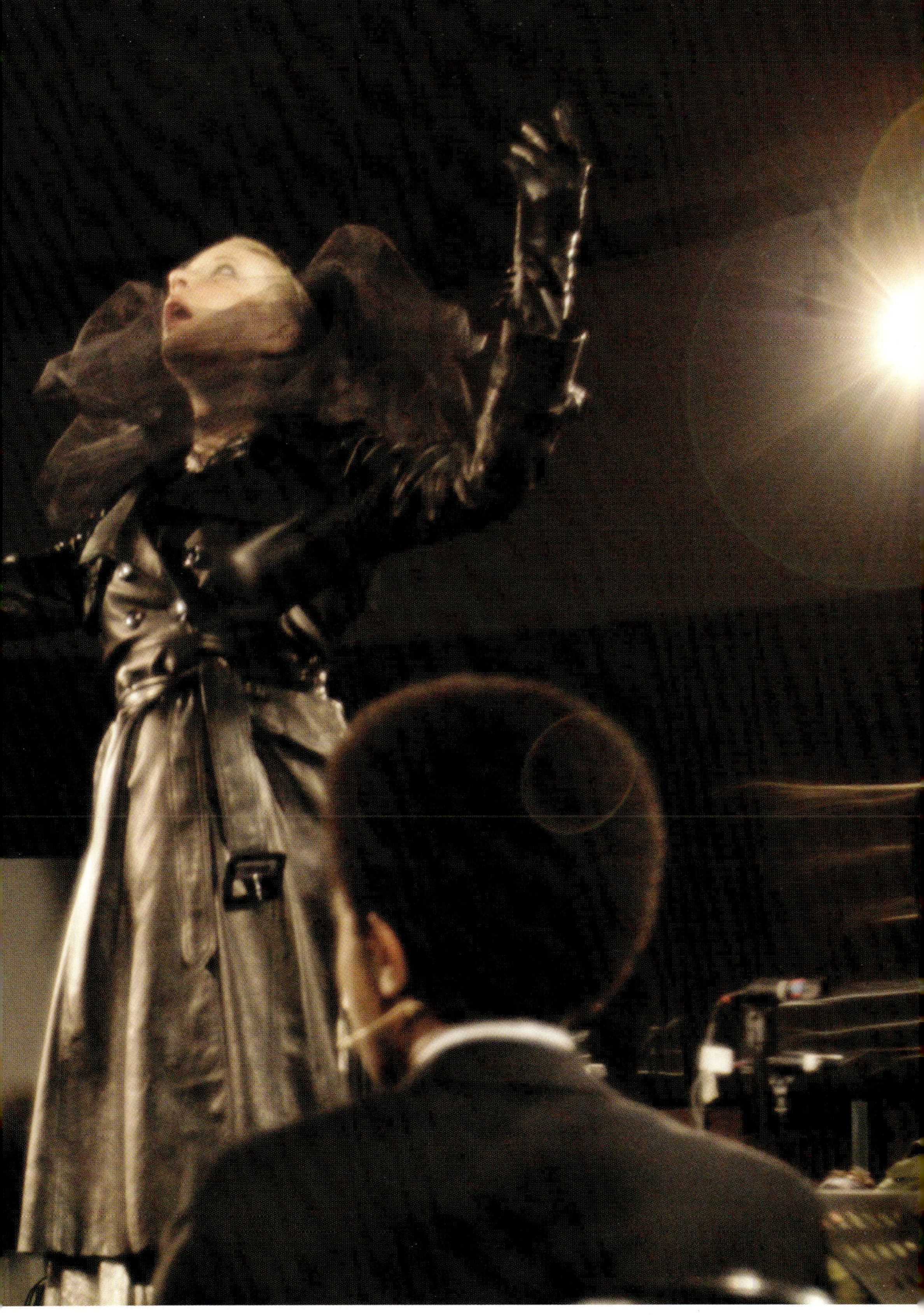

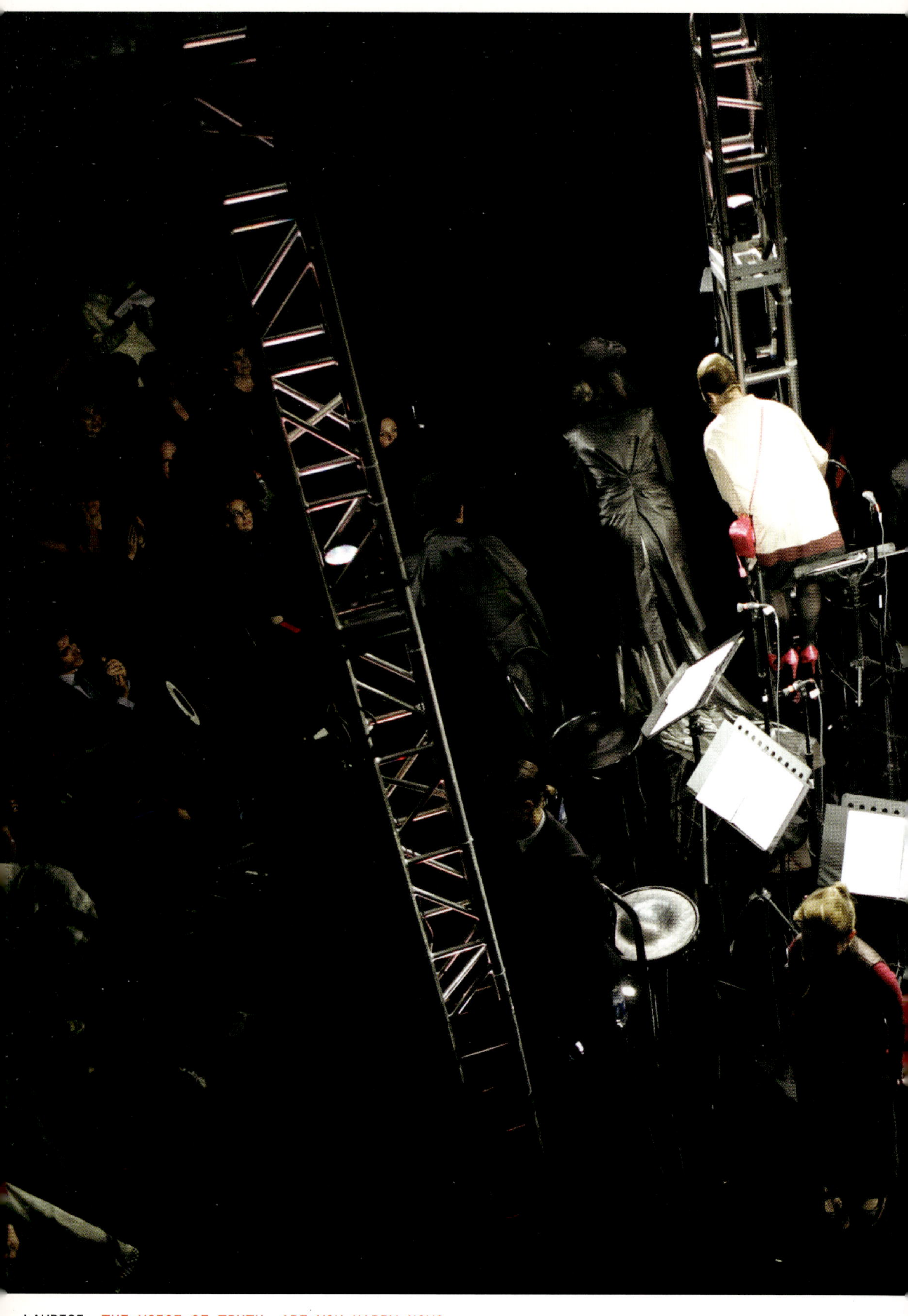

LAUDISI: THE VOICE OF TRUTH. ARE YOU HAPPY NOW?

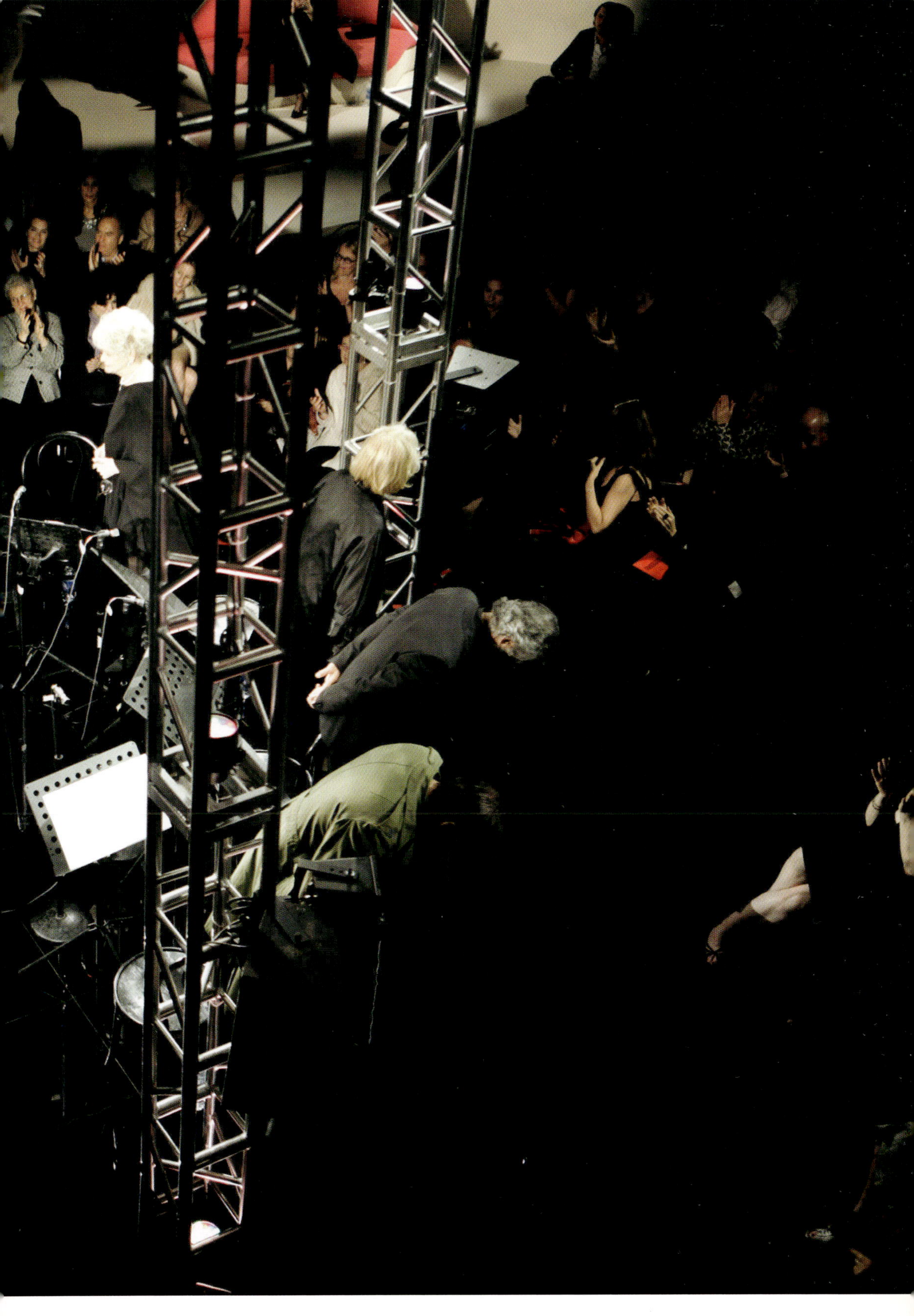

« FRANCESCO VEZZOLI AND NANCY SPECTOR IN CONVERSATION »

Nancy Spector: I remember in our discussions about your *Trailer for a Remake of Gore Vidal's Caligula* (2005) that you claimed to be responding to the unbridled excess of power being exercised by the Bush administration in the United States and abroad. The video—which also dealt with issues of ownership and intellectual property— invoked the pornography of absolute power. What are your motivations behind the production of Luigi Pirandello's *Right You Are (If You Think You Are)* from 1917? Were you responding to anything specific in our social-cultural environment or was this more an homage?

Francesco Vezzoli: Over the last few years, I produced a pilot of a reality TV show that was never aired; a trailer for a movie that did not exist; and an election campaign for two candidates that was completely fictional. With the Pirandello project my specific aim was to reproduce and mirror the kind of hysteria that seems inevitable to any contemporary art event. Therefore I decided to stage the *Premiere of a Play That Will Never Run*. (This was the original title for the performance, but I decided in the end on the simpler *One Night Only*.) The production process was similar to that of my previous projects: For *Non-Love Meetings* (2004), I contacted a company in Rome that creates pilot programs for Italian television; for *Trailer for a Remake of Gore Vidal's Caligula*, I involved a team of Hollywood producers and editors; and for *Democrazy* (2007), I worked with two of the most important political consultants in the United States. For *Right You Are…* I hired a company that usually produces events and fashion shows in New York.

I read a story a few months ago on *artforum.com* about an exhibition in a Chelsea gallery where, despite the show not being ready and the artist not being present, the gallerist decided to host the dinner anyhow. I found the situation so Pirandellian. I was intrigued that the artist, whether deliberately or not, had generated a kind of short-circuit. Pirandello's theater is generally defined by historians as "a theater of mirrors." *Right You Are…* is a play entirely focused on the identity of a certain woman and how much hype, craziness, and jealousy the mystery of her identity generates in the town where she lives. Pirandello's play felt like the perfect mirror for the schizophrenia of current artistic discourse.

NS: Actually, I attended the dinner that you speak of. The artist's exhibition was far from complete due to technical difficulties, and the decision was made to host the party, in a restaurant, even though there was no opening. The artist was supposed to attend and everyone was ready to express their sympathy or words of encouragement, but he just never showed up. Eventually we had to eat. It struck me how similar this event was to the dinners regularly hosted by gallerists at art fairs for collectors, critics, and curators, at which artists are rarely present. Everyone seems to be celebrating their access to, knowledge of, and involvement with the art, but the key element—the producer—is missing. These events are nothing if not mirrors for the privileged few to bask in their "enlightened" proximity to visual culture.

So, was it essential for you to stage *Right You Are…* in a museum? Or could you have used a regular theater? Were you deliberately targeting the art world?

FV: Yes, it was essential for me to stage *Right You Are…* in a museum and, even more, in a museum like the Guggenheim. For a project that had the surreal ambition of depicting the comedy/tragedy of life and, more specifically, life in the art world, clearly I needed a museum that in my mind resembled an Italian-style opera house. Herbert Muschamp once quoted Robert Twombly saying that at the Guggenheim "the art lover gets two shows for the price of one"—the building and the art inside it.

The night of the Pirandello project I tried to put up a show that had multiple levels, and to turn the audience into a part of the spectacle as well. In fact, the spectators were being filmed just like the actors onstage, and they could also be seen in the eight-screen, live-feed projection that was showing simultaneously in the auditorium directly beneath the rotunda. *Il pubblico* has been the focus of some of my most recent projects: that night the art-world crowd, with all its reactions and idiosyncrasies, took center stage, way beyond my expectations. Somebody suggested that the whole evening felt like an art-world set from the Robert Altman movie *Prêt à Porter*. I was really flattered by that, since I had been on set in Paris while Altman was filming. He would put Sophia Loren, say, in the front row at a real Jean-Paul Gaultier *défilé* and then take advantage of the audience's reactions by filming it live as a scene for his movie. I remember so clearly being there as a twenty-year-old, having goose bumps, and thinking that all in all it was the most amazing performance—pure genius from Altman.

NS: What you just said clarifies for me how to position the performance in a critical context. I wasn't sure initially if your commentary or critique was aimed directly at the art world per se or at the broader cult of celebrity that inflicts itself on culture. It was interesting that the unintended backdrop to your performance was Richard Prince's exhibition "Spiritual America," which in many ways alludes to this country's obsession with fame, a phenomenon that manifests itself in an overriding hunger for recognition, for that Warholian fifteen minutes. Just think, for example, about reality TV and what people will do—however ludicrous or pitiful—for a moment in the spotlight.

In terms of *Right You Are…* it was remarkable how well the audience played its prescribed role, becoming one with the production. Were you confident that this would happen? I don't think that the hour-long wait outside the museum was really planned, but it certainly intensified the atmosphere of anticipation and anxiety. The queue, which wrapped around the block, had an amazing, leveling effect because all invited guests—the elite of the art world—had to wait to get in. The Guggenheim's spiraling rotunda—the ultimate venue for people watching—also lent itself to the event's frenzied voyeurism.

In the end, it seemed quite ironic that after all the fuss about gaining entry and getting seated, the audience was asked to endure a sober, dramatic production, a real play performed by serious actors. I think people were surprised, even taken aback.

Why did you decide to stage the piece only once?

FV: I was not confident about anything before the play started. All that I knew was that I was trying to throw all these absurd and exceptional ingredients into the arena and then immortalize the resulting chemistry, the struggle between all these different powers.

This performance was never meant to be repeated, and never should be. As you correctly suggested, the audience was anxious, hysterical, and even taken aback. How can you possibly hope to recreate those feelings without the element of surprise? Perhaps this is what performance is about—expectation, fear, and the ephemerality of it all, the acknowledged impossibility of recreating the same success or failure.

The true key to the project is the sentence that I chose to open the program of the evening, which is an excerpt from a letter written by Luigi Pirandello after the premiere of the play in 1917: "It has truly been a great success. Not for the applause, but for the astonishment, the bafflement, the exasperation, and the dismay that I caused the audience. You don't know how much I enjoyed it!"

Also, given that we did not pay any of the actors and certainly not any of the celebrities to attend our "game," I think it would prove truly complicated to bring them all together again. The project, as we experienced it that night, may end up being unrepeatable simply for reasons that go well above and beyond my own aesthetic and conceptual choices.

NS: So, in the end, your classical theater piece performed in the round was performance art in the truest sense of the term. Marina Abramović said that in the early days of the genre, artists making performance adopted the principle: "No rehearsal, no repetition, no documentation."

How do you convince such accomplished and famous celebrities to participate in your artworks, especially as you say that they are not paid? Helen Mirren, Benicio del Toro, and others for *Caligula*; Sharon Stone and Bernard Henri-Levy for *Democrazy*; Natalie Portman, Cate Blanchett, and others for *Right You Are…* Sometimes I think that *this* is where the essence of your art lies.

FV: Actors and actresses are always quite intrigued and excited by my projects during our preliminary meetings. I never ask them to play a specific character and this always sounds very unusual, almost dangerous. Whatever role they end up playing, they surely know that, most of all, I want to portray and discuss their public identity. Nevertheless, most of them have accepted the challenge so far. Maybe the real reason why most of them say yes is that my projects never involve rehearsal and filming never takes longer than one day.

Every single experience is different and unique, from the moment that I speak to the "star" for the first time, until we say goodbye after what always ends up being a surreal and intense working day.

NS: Although you say you will never repeat *Right You Are…* is there anything that you would change or would do differently if the project were ever to be re-presented?

FV: In light of what I just said, it's impossible for me even to consider changing anything that happened at the Guggenheim that night. Similarly, I have never asked myself if I could have obtained better footage while I was filming *Caligula*, or if Sharon Stone could have played the candidate in any other way in *Democrazy*. If I would start thinking that way, I would lure myself into the fantasy of being a director—and I am not. At best, I am a sort of producer or sometimes just a *paparazzo*.

In the project for my first exhibition "An Embroidered Trilogy" (1997–1999), I convinced three well-known movie directors to each film and edit a video in which I played a cameo role as "the embroiderer." Back then I remember being asked to what degree I had influenced their final vision. In fact, I could have never convinced or wished to convince any of them to film in any other way other than how they did it, because the real artwork was their presence in that moment behind that camera.

Similarly, that night at the museum the real art was the gathering of all those people (artists, actors, curators, critics, journalists, and socialites) as symbols of their social and public roles and their interaction with themselves and "the art" in the most Pirandellian way possible. Once I knew that all the actors were onstage and that most of the audience had the patience to wait and watch, I felt my job was done. I just had to have the courage to let the rest happen.

«WHOEVER YOU BELIEVE ME TO BE»

MICHAEL SCHULMAN

1903 was the year Luigi Pirandello's luck turned sour. Returning from an afternoon walk, he found his wife, Antonietta, lying in bed, distraught. A flood had wiped out the sulfur mine in which the couple had invested the entirety of Antonietta's dowry. But that wasn't the worst of it—the disaster catalyzed what would become a lifelong madness in Antonietta, who became prone to fits of hysterical paranoia and was eventually institutionalized. These biographical snatches might sound familiar to anyone who has encountered *Così è (se vi pare)*, or *Right You Are (If You Think You Are)*, which Pirandello wrote fourteen years later.

The plot is set off by the arrival of three new residents in a small town: the Frola-Ponza family, which has been displaced by a terrible earthquake, and one of whom—everything hangs on the question of which—is insane. Signora Ponza has been sequestered by her husband in the top of a tall tower in a run-down courtyard. ("I shall tell you of a dream I had," the author told an audience in Buenos Aires some years later. "I saw a courtyard with no exit, and from this terrifying image was born *Right You Are (If You Think You Are)*.") Signora Frola, ostensibly her mother, is allowed to speak to her only from afar. The reason is either that Signor Ponza's first wife has died; that Signora Frola has gone mad and Signor Ponza is protecting her from the fact that the woman in the tower is in fact his second wife; or that the woman in the tower is Signora Frola's daughter after all, *Signor Ponza* is mad, and the old woman is feigning madness in order to shield his delusion that he has been married to two different women.

The earthquake may indeed recall the flood that precipitated Pirandello's troubles, and to some extent the whole back story, but it is what Hitchcock would have called a "MacGuffin," or plot device. The meat of the play is in the ravenous curiosity of the townspeople, who want to know which of these preposterous explanations is true. Laudisi, the group skeptic, smugly points out that the truth about others can't ultimately be known, but that doesn't stop them from pursuing the mystery to the point of outright persecution. And so Pirandello constructs a tantalizing paradox that unfailingly implicates the play's audience: we gaze at the performers, who in turn scrutinize the Frola-Ponzas. Although the play came a decade before Heisenberg's "uncertainty principle," which observed the unattainability of empirical truth on the subatomic level, it nevertheless acts as a sort of mathematical equation that can be applied to different kinds of data. In a 1966 Broadway revival, for instance, the townsfolk's suspicion echoed the horrors of McCarthyism, and one imagines that any society that probes the private lives of its citizens will find some resonance in the play.

Into the fray of interpretation enters Francesco Vezzoli, who transformed the play into a meditation on his perennial subject: celebrity. For Vezzoli, it was no stretch to transplant the story from its southern Italian provincial setting—he grew up in its northern equivalent—to the realm of Hollywood. Movie stars are mirrors by which we see truths about ourselves; in the process, their own truths become obscured. They forge public identities at the expense of private ones, and they are the objects of curiosity in its many varieties, from diva worship to tabloid gossip. (They are also the subjects of programs like "E! True Hollywood Story," a form Vezzoli coyly turned on himself in 2006, retelling his life as a hedonistic whirlwind of ambition, excess, and sex with call boys.) Movie stars are, for Vezzoli, a raw material, and his *Right You Are...* had no shortage of them.

Hype—another stepchild of curiosity—is also a raw material, and the event that took place at the Guggenheim on October 27, 2007, was rich with it. At thirty minutes past the advertised start time, a crowd of film stars, art-world luminaries, gawkers, groupies, and the merely curious was still waiting anxiously in a line around the block. The doors opened, finally, onto a series of concentric circles: a circular black stage in the center of the rotunda, surrounded by seating and, in the tiers of the Guggenheim spiral, standing room for a second group of spectators, who were handed binoculars as they came in. (Vezzoli no doubt anticipated that these audience members, a contemporary version of the Elizabethan groundlings, would immediately use their binoculars to check out the A-list crowd below.) A third segment of the audience was relegated to the downstairs auditorium, where live-stream video projected the actors' faces onto a split screen, a device that recalled both "Hollywood Squares" and surveillance tapes.

The first thing that should be said about the performance was that it was not exactly audience-friendly. Vezzoli presented the evening not as a full theatrical staging, but rather as a reading, with the actors seated in a circle facing inwards so that no single spectator could see them all head-on. (Unless, that is, you were watching it all on video in the auditorium, in which case you might have ended up with the best seats in the house.) Secondly, if you had come expecting bravura performances, you would have been disappointed. While Vezzoli was careful to choose celebrities with bona fide acting credibility, he did not 'direct' them. In the scant rehearsal time that was available that same afternoon he had not given acting notes. Instead, the actors were left to interpret their roles in an unstructured, improvisatory manner. As a result, none of the traditional nuances of stage acting—dramatic highs and lows, comic timing—was evident as they read from their scripts. Dianne Wiest brought her trademark quiet neurosis to Amalia Agazzi; Peter Sarsgaard, as her brother, had a fussy charm; while Abigail Breslin imbued Dina, the youngest of the busybodies, with brash inquisitiveness. All of them, however, were muted by the cavernousness of the space and the insularity of the stage set-up. (Although Elaine Stritch, displaying her seasoned Broadway chops, was able to cut through some of the ether as the obnoxious Signora Cini).

And then there was Natalie Portman, as Laudisi. At first glance, Laudisi appears to be the play's voice of reason and the most likely stand-in for the author or director. He is the only character to see the game of truth seeking for what it is: futile. Each of the play's three acts ends with his gloating laughter, as his theories of relative truth are consistently proven correct. The audience, considering itself as knowing and above-it-all as Laudisi, is inclined to identify with him. But this Laudisi came in the form of a female movie star—one notable for her delicate feminine features—dressed in a Prada suit and sporting a fake moustache. Casting Laudisi as a woman in drag served as a distancing device, and it hinted that, for Vezzoli, Laudisi is not the stand-in at all, but rather a character to be viewed critically along with all the rest. Portman's Laudisi, like the world he describes, was not to be taken at face value; his certainty about uncertainty was no longer a source of comfort.

While, in a traditional staging of *Right You Are…*, Laudisi would dominate the action, there was nothing particularly commanding about Portman's performance. Like the others, she played more to the camera lens in front of her than to the live audience. The remoteness of the actors, while frustrating, was purposeful. Ultimately, the event was not intended as a night at the theater, but as the idea of a theater piece set at an observable remove. The most conspicuous clue that the concept of theater was itself under investigation was the presence of Anita Ekberg, perched on Salvador Dalí's *Mae West Lips Sofa* at the base of the spiral. A prime specimen of the kind of aging European film icon Vezzoli has used obsessively in his work, Ekberg was told simply to watch, and, for the most part, she did. Ekberg's special appearance made her both an object and an active participant in a communal act of voyeurism. Watching her, we were prompted to think about celebrity, and about watching celebrities as they watch each other. At times, it seemed as if the actors on stage were holding a private rehearsal or having a conversation among themselves.

Into this band of movie stars came two sorrowful outsiders—also movie stars, of course. As Signora Frola, Ellen Burstyn gave an affectingly vulnerable performance, while David Strathairn brought a buttoned-up anguish to Signor Ponza. As each character pleaded to be recognized as sane, neither actor implied overt madness, which is as it should be. More than anything, Signora Frola and Signor Ponza seemed pitiful, desperate to evade the questioning of their neighbors. "We are forced to tell stories that nobody believes," the fraught Signora Frola tells her interrogators, in one of the evening's many nods to the perils of celebrity.

In the play's final act, Laudisi, who turns out to be more mischievous than wise, suggests that the woman in question, the enigmatic Signora Ponza, be summoned from her tower to settle the issue of her identity. ("Expect a ghost," he warns the others.) It is her arrival that gave Pirandello—and Vezzoli—occasion for a *coup de théâtre*. The stage lights that had been rigged in the Guggenheim flickered wildly, accompanied by the sound of howling wind, and Cate Blanchett—dressed in Dior, flanked by fake paparazzi, and every inch a movie star—began her ravishing descent down the spiral path. Finally, she took her rightful and inevitable place at the center of the stage and, with a preternatural poise that instantly brought to mind roles like Elizabeth I and Galadriel, proclaimed:

"The truth is simply this: I am Signora Frola's daughter. And I am Signore Ponza's second wife. I am both and—alone. In my tower—I am Nobody... I am neither, I am either, I am no one, I am anyone. I am whoever you believe me to be."

With these lines, Blanchett threw her head back to the heavens, stretching her arms out like a conductor. Remarkably, she managed to play to every audience member in the house; even to those in the upper reaches of the Guggenheim, she was visible and immediate. Signora Ponza's brief appearance is bound to be haunting: she is the object of the gaze gazing back, the avatar of unknowability announcing itself with a shout. But Blanchett was altogether uncanny. Her performance was at the heart of Vezzoli's project, and it became clear that Signora Ponza, not Laudisi, represented the voice of the artist.

Movie stars, of course, are "whoever" we believe them to be, in film and in the gossip pages, but Vezzoli's take on Signora Ponza wasn't as facile as that. As a celebrity artist in a culture that increasingly treats artists as commodities—and as the product of a provincial childhood—Vezzoli must know what it means to be defined by the perceptions of others. As early as his embroidered portraits of gay icons like Liza Minnelli and Maria Callas (1999), his work has been situated at the nexus of glamour and solitude. Beneath the glitz of his *Right You Are...* was a kernel of heartache: a private pain that thirsts for, but is not healed by, public exposure.

Pirandello, who himself became an object of scrutiny due to his wife's condition, also had something to say about heartache in *Right You Are...*, although he gave it the relatively benign façade of a philosophical riddle. In Act II, Signora Frola plays a somber tune on the piano, which Pirandello indicated should be an aria from Giovanni Paisiello's opera *Nina, o sia La pazza per amore (Nina, or the Girl Driven Mad by Love)*. Vezzoli was true to the stage directions, using excerpts from *Nina...* both in this scene and at the beginning of each act. It was one of several touches that suggested identification with the play beyond mere publicity baiting. For Vezzoli, a play about an unknown woman in a Sicilian village could also be a play about movie stars and Miuccia Prada. After all, the bridge existed in his own life. Ask any gay boy from a small town, and he'll tell you that it's possible to feel more kinship with a diva on an old record than with the next-door neighbors, and that creating an identity for public consumption, whether you are Anita Ekberg, Cate Blanchett, or "Nobody," is a sad, mad affair.

Contributors

RoseLee Goldberg is the founding director of Performa, a bi-annual festival of
performance in New York City, inaugurated in 2004. She is author of Performance
Art: From Futurism to the Present and Laurie Anderson, a monograph. She teaches at
New York University and writes regularly on contemporary international performance.

Herbert Muschamp was a prominent architecture critic and author. He began writing for
various magazines, including Vogue, House and Garden, Artforum and The New Republic.
Muschamp became the architecture critic for the The New York Times in 1992. Among
other features, he wrote the "Icons" column for T: The New York Times Style Magazine.

Jason Schmidt is a New York based photographer. His first book Artists, a collection
of portraits of contemporary artists was published in 2006. He is a frequent
contributor to the New York Times Magazine.

Michael Schulman is on the editorial staff of The New Yorker, where he contributes
to "The Talk of the Town" and "Goings On About Town." His work has also appeared
in The New York Sun and The Believer.

Nancy Spector is Chief Curator at the Solomon R. Guggenheim Museum, New York. She
writes frequently on contemporary art.

Matthias Vriens is a celebrated photographer best known as a contributor to culture
and fashion magazines, including The New York Times Magazine, Men's Vogue, Vanity
Fair, Elle and GQ. His work has been exhibited internationally, including two solo
shows at The Project, New York; the Moderna Museet, Stockholm; and the Nederlands
Foto Instituut, Rotterdam.

«

I DECIDED TO STAGE THE PREMIERE OF A PLAY THAT WAS NEVER GOING TO RUN.

»

"IT HAS TRULY BEEN A GREAT SUCCESS. NOT FOR THE
APPLAUSE, BUT FOR THE ASTONISHMENT, THE BAFFLEMENT,
THE EXASPERATION AND THE DISMAY I CAUSED THE
AUDIENCE. YOU DON'T KNOW HOW MUCH I ENJOYED IT!"

- Luigi Pirandello
(letter to his sister Lina after the premiere of Right You
Are (If You Think You Are), 18 June 1917)

Francesco Vezzoli has undertaken a new adaptation of
Luigi Pirandello's infamous 1917 play Right You Are
(If You Think You Are). Conceived by Pirandello as a
parable on the impossibility of objective truth, the
play has been transformed by Vezzoli into a stirring
meditation on our culture's obsession with fame and
the private world of the film star. Along the way,
Vezzoli has assembled an extraordinary cast, who have
embraced his visionary approach toward the material.
Vezzoli examines the fundamental ambiguity of truth,
the seductive powers of language, and the instability
of the human persona.

Right You Are (If You Think You Are) orients itself
around the elusive character of Signora Ponza, a
woman who exists only through the eyes of others.
Constructed as a series of conversations among a
group of provincial Italians, the play turns on their
dissection of Signora Ponza and her family, skewering
the social forces of gossip in the process. The
boundaries between illusion and reality, surface and
depth are inextricably obscured as the group becomes
increasingly frenzied in their attempt to discover
the true identity of their absent subject.

Vezzoli's recent video works Trailer for a Remake of
Gore Vidal's "Caligula" (2005), Marlene Redux: A True
Hollywood Story! (2006), and Democrazy (2007) take
public identity as their subject. Now, in his
first-ever live performance, this theme will
literally take center stage.

Please note: strobe lighting is used during performance.

A PERFORMA07 COMMISSION
PRODUCED BY GAGOSIAN GALLERY
IN COLLABORATION WITH PERFORMA AND
THE SOLOMON R. GUGGENHEIM FOUNDATION

Project by FRANCESCO VEZZOLI

Produced by GAGOSIAN GALLERY
Producer VALENTINA CASTELLANI
Art Director MATTHIAS VRIENS
Artistic Producer LUCA CORBETTA

Starring
(in alphabetical order)

CATE BLANCHETT	Signora Ponza
ABIGAIL BRESLIN	Dina
ELLEN BURSTYN	Signora Frola
MARCUS CARL FRANKLIN	Announcer/Mayor
NATALIE PORTMAN	Laudisi
PETER SARSGAARD	Agazzi
DAVID STRATHAIRN	Signor Ponza
ELAINE STRITCH	Signora Cini
DIANNE WIEST	Amalia Agazzi

With special appearance by
ANITA EKBERG

Text adaptation by ANDREW UPTON
Script consultant MARA CHIARETTI

Cate Blanchett's costume designed by
JOHN GALLIANO

Natalie Portman's costume designed by
MIUCCIA PRADA

FRANCESCO VEZZOLI
ONE NIGHT ONLY
RIGHT YOU ARE
IF YOU THINK YOU ARE
By Luigi Pirandello, 1917

Saturday, October 27, 2007

Executive Producer: Brian Phillips
Casting Directors: Laura Rosenthal and Ali Farrell
Video Production: Daniel Desure
Production Manager: Elinyisia Mosha
Stage Manager: Rachel Perlman
Lighting Design: JKLD
Sound Design: Audible Difference, Inc.
Set Designer: Scott Pask
Set Production: Darren Kraft, Brian Kraft,
and Gary Ford
Technical Advisor: Harry Lee
Video Coordinator: Scharff Weisberg
Props: Johnny Hardesty and Gina Volpe
Casting Associate: Maribeth Fox
Production Assistant: Justin Conner
Graphic Design: Goto Design, New York

GAGOSIAN GALLERY

Larry Gagosian, Valentina Castellani,
Alison McDonald, Nicole Heck, Laura Hamdan,
Louise Neri, Melissa Lazarov, and Andisheh Avini

PERFORMA07

RoseLee Goldberg, Esa Nickle, Defne Ayas, Lana Wilson,
Tairone Bastien, Ute Zimmermann, Sara Dufour, Cian McConn,
and Kirsty Carter

SOLOMON R. GUGGENHEIM MUSEUM

Nancy Spector, Nat Trotman, Michael Lavin, Maria Celi,
Stephen Diefenderfer, Betsy Ennis, Sara Geelan, Abigail
Lawler, Jessica Ludwig, Sari Sharaby, Steve Ursell, Helen
Warwick, Ben Whine, Paul Bridge, Mary Ann Hoag, Anna
Lavatelli, Michael Sarff, and Melanie Taylor

Costume for Cate Blanchett has been generously
provided by Christian Dior Couture.
Thanks to Katherine Ross and Alexis Roche.
Special thanks to Verde Visconti and
Antonella Lapetina at Prada.

Dedicated to HERBERT MUSCHAMP.

«

THAT NIGHT THE ART-WORLD CROWD, WITH ALL ITS REACTIONS AND IDIOSYNCRASIES, TOOK CENTER STAGE, WAY BEYOND MY EXPECTATIONS.

»

FRANCESCO VEZZOLI

Luigi Pirandello (1867–1936) is the most celebrated Italian dramatist and author of the twentieth century.

Along with Henrik Ibsen and August Strindberg, Pirandello revolutionized modern drama in all its aspects, from staging to dialogue to the form of the play. His works, infused with a peculiar brand of humor, generally portray Italian middle-class society. Analytical in nature and for the most part lacking in action, they are dialectical disquisitions on essence and appearance, illusion and reality, the problem of personal identity, and the impossibility of objective truth and honest communication. His dramatic oeuvre (forty-three plays in all) illustrates his relativistic and pessimistic tenets and philosophical beliefs.

Among Pirandello's best-known works are the novel _Uno, nessuno e centomila_ (One, No One and One Hundred Thousand) and the plays _Sei personaggi in cerca d'autore_ (Six Characters in Search of an Author), _Questa sera si recita a soggetto_ (Tonight We Improvise), _Enrico IV_ (Henry IV), _Il gioco delle parti_ (The Rules of the Game), _Come mi vuoi_ (As You Desire Me), and _Così é, se vi pare_ (Right You Are, If You Think You Are). He published a collection of five plays under the title _Maschere nude_ (Naked Masks). His most famous novel is _Il fu Mattia Pascal_ (The Late Mattia Pascal).

Pirandello's works are regularly staged, revived, and studied in Europe. Although occasionally produced on and off Broadway, his dramatic works have not, for the most part, found enduring favor with American playgoers.

Pirandello was awarded the Nobel Prize in Literature in 1934.

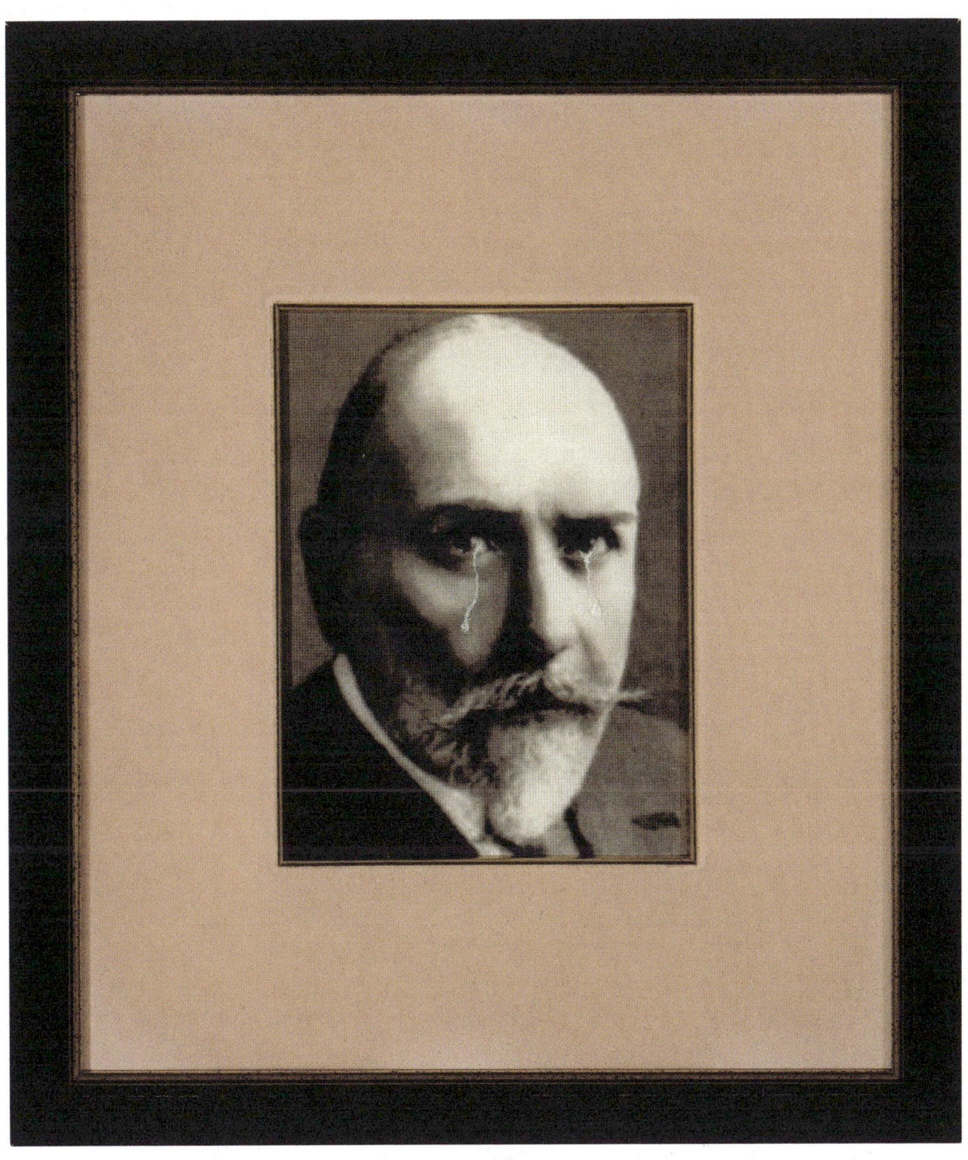

FRANCESCO VEZZOLI *Uno, nessuno e centomila* (One, No One and One Hundred Thousand), 2007, Laserprint on canvas with metallic embroidery in artist's frame, 16 ½ x 14 inches, 41.9 x 35.6 cm

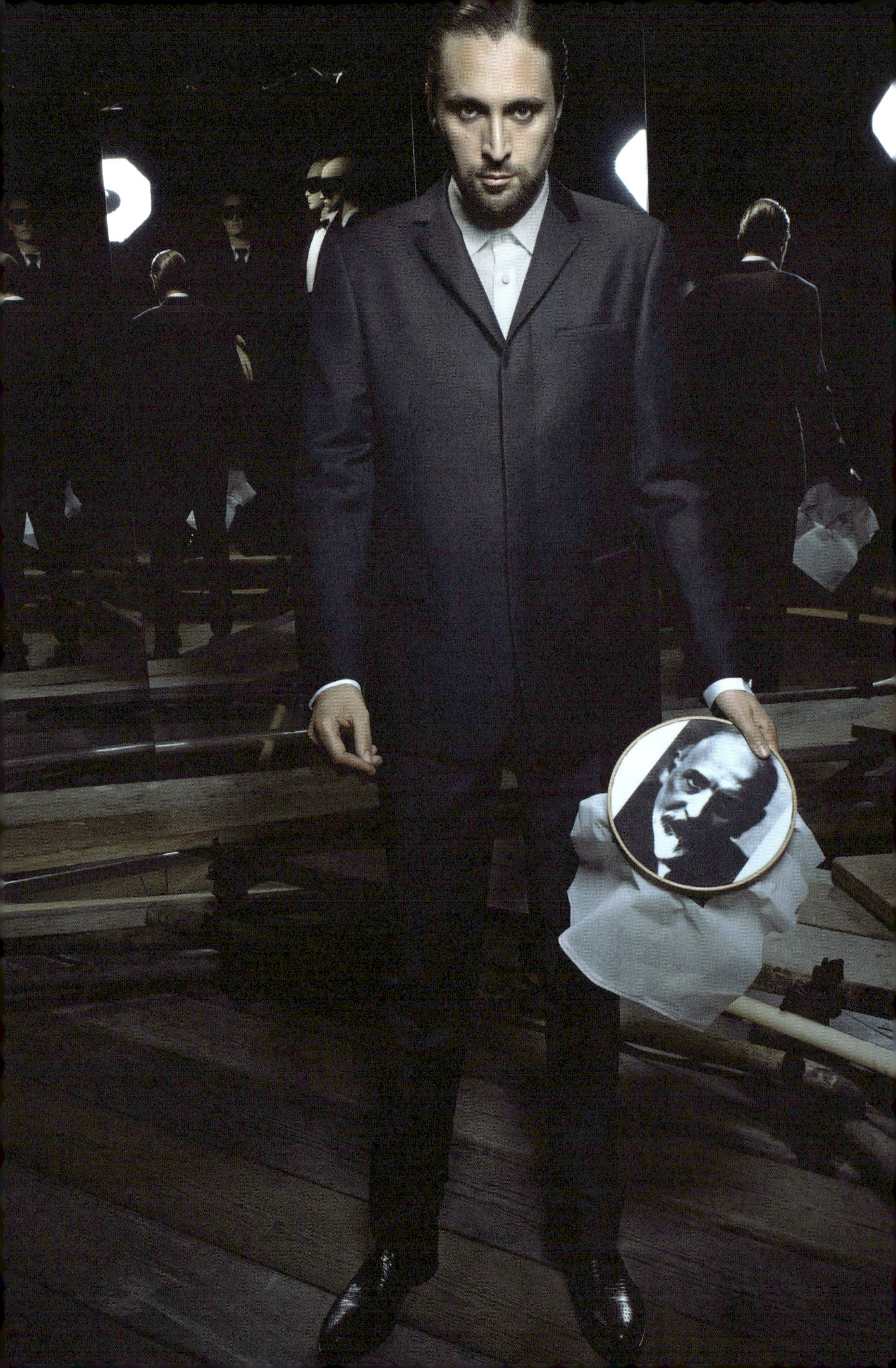

Born in Brescia, Italy, in 1971, Francesco Vezzoli attended the Central Saint Martins College of Art and Design in London, where he received a BA in 1995. His intense and visually provocative work, which includes video installations, petit-point embroideries, and photography, mixes heterogeneous languages and genres and brings together references to pop icons, auteur cinema, art history, and social and private issues.

In 2003 Vezzoli began a study of the media-dominated language of contemporary culture. His latest projects include Non-Love Meetings (2004), a reality dating game inspired by poet and director Pier Paolo Pasolini (starring Catherine Deneuve, Jeanne Moreau, and Marianne Faithfull, presented at Fondazione Prada in Milan); Amàlia Traïda (2004), an imaginary soap opera about Portuguese singer and queen of fado Amália Rodrigues (with Sonia Braga and Lauren Bacall, produced by Fundação Serralves); and Trailer for a Remake of Gore Vidal's Caligula (2005), a parody of contemporary Hollywood aesthetic standards (starring Gore Vidal, Helen Mirren, Milla Jovovich, and Courtney Love, among others).

Vezzoli has had solo shows at Fondazione Prada, Milan; Castello di Rivoli, Turin; New Museum, New York; The Power Plant, Toronto; Pinakothek der Moderne, Munich; Museu Serralves, Porto; Tate Modern, London; Galerie für Zeitgenössische Kunst, Leipzig; and Le Consortium, Dijon. His video projects and needleworks have been presented at the Istanbul Biennial (1999), Venice Biennale (2001 and 2005), São Paulo Bienal (2004), Whitney Biennial (2006), Taipei Biennial (2006), and Shanghai Biennale (2006). He has participated in group shows at numerous institutions, including Whitechapel Art Gallery, London; Palazzo Grassi, Venice; P.S.1 Contemporary Art Center, New York; Hirshhorn Museum and Sculpture Garden, Washington, D.C.; The Studio Museum in Harlem, New York; The Fabric Workshop and Museum, Philadelphia; Grand Palais, Paris; Witte de With, Rotterdam; Tate Liverpool; Migros Museum, Zurich; MAMbo, Bologna; and MAXXI, Rome.

Metro-Gol
PRESENTS
Greta
AS YOU L
MELVYN DOUGLAS
OWEN
A George Fitzm

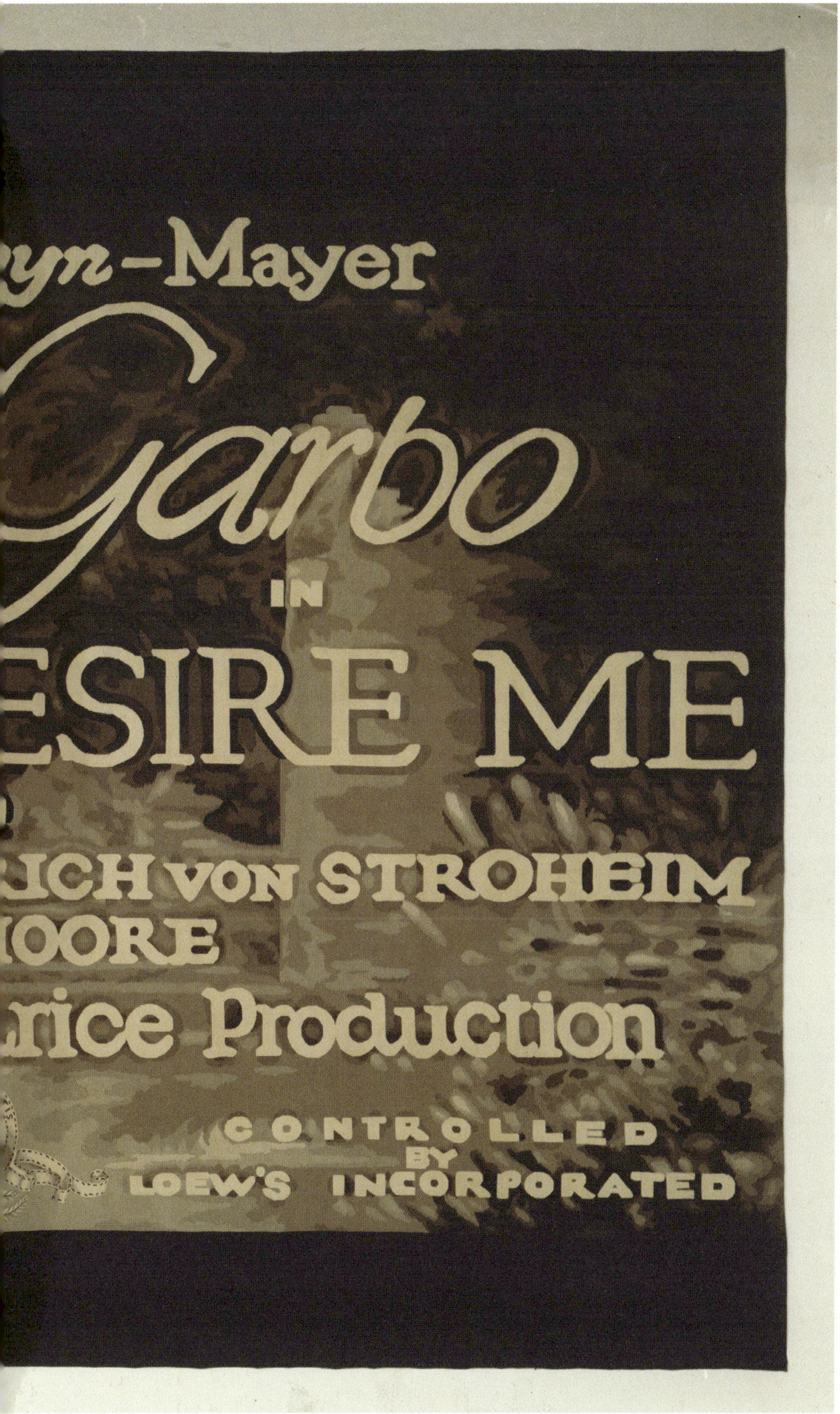

FRANCESCO VEZZOLI *Sono Come Tu Mi Vuoi* (As You Desire Me), 2007, Handmade wool gobelin tapestry, 177 ¹/₄ x 236 ¹/₄ inches, 460 x 600 cm

«

I AM NEITHER,
I AM EITHER,
I AM NO ONE,
I AM ANYONE.
I AM WHOEVER YOU
BELIEVE ME TO BE.

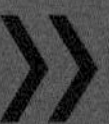

»